BIRDMANIA

BERND BRUNNER

Foreword by **PETE DUNNE**

Translation by **JANE BILLINGHURST**

BIRDMANIA

A Remarkable Passion for Birds

GREYSTONE BOOKS

Vancouver/Berkeley

Originally published by Verlag Galiani Berlin, Germany, as *Ornithomania: Geschichte einer besonderen Leidenschaft* by Bernd Brunner copyright © 2015 by Verlag Kiepenheuer & Witsch, Cologne
Revised text for the English edition copyright © 2017 by Bernd Brunner
English translation copyright © 2017 by Jane Billinghurst
Foreword copyright © 2017 by Pete Dunne
Illustrations copyright © as credited
First published by Greystone Books in 2017

17 18 19 20 21 6 5 4 3 2

Greystone Books Ltd.
www.greystonebooks.com

Cataloguing data available from Library and Archives Canada
ISBN 978-1-77164-277-4 (cloth)
ISBN 978-1-77164-278-1 (epub)

Copyediting by Lesley Cameron
Jacket and interior design by Nayeli Jimenez
Front cover illustration: *Sclater's Cassowary* by John Gerrard Keulemans
Back cover illustration: *Juan Fernández Firecrown* by René Primevère Lesson
Front flap illustration: *Little Owls* by Johann Conrad Susemihl

Printed and bound in Canada on ancient-forest-friendly paper by Friesens.

We gratefully acknowledge the financial support of the Canada Council for the Arts, the British Columbia Arts Council, the Province of British Columbia through the Book Publishing Tax Credit, and the Government of Canada through the Canada Book Fund for our publishing activities.

The translation of this work was supported by a grant from the Goethe-Institut, which is funded by the German Ministry of Foreign Affairs.

Canadä

 BRITISH COLUMBIA   BRITISH COLUMBIA ARTS COUNCIL
An agency of the Province of British Columbia

 Canada Council   Conseil des arts
for the Arts   du Canada

 GOETHE INSTITUT

Table of Contents

Foreword

—————

SINCE BEFORE OUR ancestors surrendered perch space in the limbs of trees, birds have played an integral role in our lives. Serving first as heralds of approaching danger, birds went on to become augurs of fortune, even emissaries of our gods (and in some cultures the personification of gods themselves). In more recent times birds have served as indicators of environmental health, our canaries in the coal mine. Bernd Brunner's fascinating and comprehensive book explores the many ways birds have figured in the human experience and why so many among us have made birds the centerpiece of our lives.

Must you, then, be a bird watcher to enjoy this book? No. As birds have demonstrated throughout human history, all humans need bring to this enduring interspecific relationship is awareness. The engaging power of birds does the rest.

But why this animal group? Of all the creatures on the planet, only our domestic pets garner more human favor than do these feathered creatures. Birds delight us with their colors, enchant us with their songs, and reward our studied regard with their uncommon patience. While other animals flee at our approach, birds treat us with tolerance, knowing that their powers of flight give them control over the situation.

And here, I think, lies the key to our love of birds. There are few creatures on earth that we humans must look up to. Birds in both a literal and figurative sense command our lofty regard, forcing us to see them with eyes raised as they exercise their enviable powers of flight. Is it any wonder, then, that birds have long been held as our link to the heavens? As the author of North America's first true field guide, Roger Tory Peterson, so often observed, the only creatures with feathered wings are angels and birds. Dr. Peterson earned his wings on July 28, 1996.

As a bird watcher, it has been my privilege to study birds on every continent, an accomplishment that not only underscores my level of interest but also highlights the adaptive capacity of birds whose wings have allowed them to colonize and flourish everywhere on this planet. No other creatures so deserve the title "citizens of Earth," inhabiting as they do, every habitat under the sun: from blue skies to blue seas, from the most moisture-impoverished corners of our globe to the most inhospitable polar regions. Birds have even made themselves at home in urban and suburban environs, habitats modified solely to meet our species' needs. In fact, there has never been a time in human history when more people have lived in greater intimacy with birds, and it was precisely this burgeoning intimacy that led to my own lifelong fascination with birds. In the 1950s, suburbia was still a social experiment. As it turned out, this hybrid environment, which came into being at the end of World War II, was one where birds and humans could (and still can) flourish together.

Bird watching is now North America's second most popular outdoor activity (second only to gardening). I trace the late twentieth-century explosion in its popularity precisely to the suburban sprawl that brought tens of millions of North American residents into

day-to-day intimacy with robins, mockingbirds, jays, and other emissaries of the natural world. I trace my personal fascination just as precisely to a birthday present given to a neighborhood friend, whose gift of binoculars coupled with a pocket-sized field guide to birds brought Donna and me intimacy and insight that turned ordinary suburban yards into portals of discovery and wonder.

Birds have the power to transform human lives, as the many accounts collected in this book attest. And while I never personally collected birds' eggs—the focus of chapter 13—I did, in my youth, seek out birds' nests to marvel at the color and complexity of the near-perfect vessels of procreation cradled within. Having done so, I can easily see why egg collecting was pursued with such passion. So prized were the eggs of the peregrine that during the DDT era, when raptor populations plummeted, a twenty-four-hour guard was placed at some easily accessed aeries in the United Kingdom. One look at a peregrine egg, whose cinnamon-colored base is overlaid with dark spotting of fathomless complexity, is enough to ignite the acquisitive instincts of any lover of beauty. And while I never encountered breeding peregrines in my youth—suburbia is not the falcons' preferred habitat—my suburban-calibrated eyes beheld other orb-shaped treasures as alluring as the eggs of the peregrine. Orbs like the summer sky–blue eggs of American robins, cradled in their adobe nests, and the twilight-blue eggs of gray catbirds whose twig nests were often placed within reach of seven-year-old arms.

And while you may never have indulged in bird study as seriously as those characters who figure in this book, it is certain that birds have touched your life. If you were, perchance, a baseball fan, as all young American boys (and many young American girls) of my generation were, it is certain that you kept up with the league standings of the Toronto Blue Jays, the St. Louis Cardinals, and the Baltimore Orioles, as the teams would be listed in phylogenetic order if the American Ornithological Society, instead of the baseball commissioner, were managing the lineup. But by the age of ten, I'd stopped collecting baseball cards and obsessed instead upon the collecting (or listing) of birds, accounting the finding of a scarlet tanager or Kentucky warbler as gratifying as the acquisition of a Mickey Mantle or Roger Maris baseball card.

Even if you are not a sports fan, you cannot help but be touched by birds, festooned as they are upon half the holiday cards sent and received in this country. And it is almost certain that you are familiar with the old Christmas folk ballad "The Twelve Days of Christmas." Were you never impressed that six of the gifts presented by the author's "true love" were birds? Possibly seven, insofar as the "five gold rings" in the song are widely believed to be not precious metal but gold finches, a gift more within the means of humble folk in Europe at that time.

To this day, the inexpensive nature of bird watching remains one of the avocation's most compelling attributes. Whereas a round of golf might cost $100, access to most natural areas is free. The purchase of entry-level binoculars and a field guide to birds can be made for less than a single round of golf and sets you on a course of discovery that begins in your backyard, and then sweeps you to the farthest reaches of the planet. You are now in danger of becoming, as chapter 15 describes, one of the tens of millions of people who are "Mad for Bird Watching."

There are approximately ten thousand species of birds on the planet and no single individual has seen them all. You could be first and secure a place among the ranks of the ornithological greats treated in this engaging and informative book. Or you could content yourself with celebrating and observing birds closer to home, an activity that would also earn you an honorable mention in the ranks of the bird lovers gathered here.

PETE DUNNE, New Jersey Audubon Ambassador for Birding

What's That Sound?

I F YOU'RE NOT outside right now, take a moment to open a window. What do you hear? The rumble of engines? And behind the dull roar of civilization? Human voices? Muffled undercurrents of sound? Dogs barking? Cats yowling? Insects buzzing? Anything else? Do you get the impression that there's twittering going on? Chirping, warbling, fluttering? There's a good chance you do, because there are an estimated 200 billion to 400 billion birds in the world. If you wait a moment and then listen again carefully, you might well notice that something has changed in the interplay between the sounds the birds are making and the general mood outside. It depends on the time of day, the temperature, and a multitude of other factors. Sometimes a cloud passing across the face of the sun is enough to silence the birds. Or a gust of wind might come along and suddenly throw them all into a panic.

There are people for whom all this twittering is not enough. They don't want to just hear the noises from afar; they want to get closer to the birds making these sounds. They want to observe them and investigate the rhythms of their lives, discover their migration routes, feed them, enjoy their company, gain control over them, or even try to kill them—perhaps because they cannot get over the fact that birds, with their ability to fly, are capable of something that will be forever beyond any human's grasp. Their preoccupation with birds allows them to transcend the limitations of their own world.

Strictly speaking, birds are nothing more than winged verte-brates with beaks. As Jonathan Weiner wrote in *The Beak of the Finch,* "Beaks are to birds what hands are to us." Yet birds are made of lighter stuff than we are. They breathe faster, their body tempera-ture is higher, and their bones are filled with air. They can be found in many different guises everywhere on Earth—and they predate us by some 160 million years. Many species are considered to be particularly graceful, and some have beautiful colors or fascinating feathers. Sometimes they produce sounds that people call "songs." Almost all are capable of achieving lift-off and flying, acting as intermediaries between heaven and earth as they thread their way through the sky without leaving a trace. They allow themselves to be carried on updrafts; they coast in spirals, flit, twirl, careen, or simply sweep serenely through the air; and when they fly in a flock, they do so in varying formations: cranes and wild geese in Vs, oys-ter catchers and curlews often in a line, and starlings in hosts that move in concert as if directed by an invisible conductor.

And what about the people who abandon themselves to birds? Some give up successful careers to devote themselves to their study; others dream so often about encountering the rare birds they desire to see that they end up believing they have set eyes on them. Phi-losophers, musicians, and writers incorporate them into their work. Many who are seduced by birds wrestle for recognition; others seek neither fame nor fortune, never put pen to paper, and focus instead on cultivating intimate relationships with their beloved birds. Yet others extend their passion to include other animals, and it is no surprise that these are often other winged creatures such as butter-flies, bees and other beneficial insects, or bats.

It's easy for observers to project human experiences onto birds and get incredibly emotional about them. At a deeper level, however, people who devote themselves to birds open themselves up to the beauty of creatures that live their lives according to mysterious, alien laws. It's almost as though birds inhabit an alternative reality. Despite the divide—or perhaps because of it—engaging with them brings many people great joy.

A passion for birds often goes hand in hand with scientific ambition; in its most extreme manifestations, it can be a downright obsession. When everything else is going off the rails, birders can forget personal issues and money worries as collecting, observing, or trapping birds takes priority. Such fervor can fuel the discovery of new species and research into what makes birds the way they are. It can make people want to hold birds captive so they can observe them, which runs counter to the fundamental needs of the birds themselves—particularly those that are capable of flight. The satisfaction some bird aficionados derive from being able to care for birds, to protect them from the threats posed by civilization, is huge.

The author Jonathan Rosen, who watches birds from his apartment by New York's Central Park, might well have been correct when he wrote that "everyone is a birdwatcher, but there are two kinds of birdwatchers: those who know what they are and those who haven't yet realized it."

Bird watching—sometimes associated with drawing up what is known as a "life list" (a record of all birds either seen or heard)—has recently become a popular pastime. It is a hobby for which millions of people spare no effort or expense. No weather conditions are too awful, no time of the day or night too inconvenient to indulge in this passion. Bird watchers know that birds are everywhere; all you have to do is look out of the window or, better yet, step outside.

Although many people are bewitched by birds, some find these flighty creatures trigger phobias, which in an extreme form can lead to downright hatred. During the latter part of the nineteenth century, Giovanni Salvadori, an Italian priest and doctor who had revered bird hunting from a young age, campaigned with missionary zeal for the eradication of songbirds because—in his opinion—they threatened insects, which he felt were much more important to humankind. "Protect insects and embrace bird hunting," he exhorted at the First International Congress of Ornithologists in Vienna in 1884, a clarion call that gained him support in certain circles.

Then there are people who find birds unnerving because their movements are so erratic. As Alfred Hitchcock's classic movie *The*

Birds reminds us, flocks of birds can be menacing—and their random, aggressive behavior unhinges the main character in the film. Remember, too, the office at the awful Bates Motel in *Psycho,* where the mere presence of silent stuffed birds signals impending doom. There's a reason we refer to a "murder" of crows.

This book is about people who have been involved with birds in myriad ways. My choice of characters is subjective, and the content is not as neatly compartmentalized as the chapter titles suggest. The selections are not a comprehensive overview; they are merely a sample, a *tour d'horizon,* of many different bird lovers out there. Some have earned their place among the ranks of ornithologists and have made important contributions to science. Others are not part of the great project to advance shared knowledge of birds internationally but have dedicated themselves instead to a single bird or to an issue or idea somehow connected with birds. You find people who love birds no matter where you look, and it is my pleasure to reacquaint you with some you will already know and introduce you to others whose stories you may seldom—or perhaps never—have heard.

{ 1 }

Early Enthusiasts

B IRDS HAVE BEEN present in our lives and thoughts for a very long time. At Chauvet Cave in France, next to drawings of a diverse assortment of mammals dating back to the last ice age, there is an owl. The ancient Egyptians imagined entering eternity equipped with wings, and they offered hundreds of thousands of mummified falcons to their gods. The Greeks connected Aphrodite, their goddess of love, with doves, and believed that the owls that lived in the beams of the Parthenon high up on the Acropolis brought good luck. The use of small owls as decoys (they attract songbirds that are driven to mob them) probably dates back to the Bronze Age; carrier pigeons were popular in India, Persia, and Egypt. We know the Aztecs worshipped the red-and-green feathered quetzal as the "god of the winds." Some indigenous peoples in North America, especially in the Pacific Northwest, venerate the thunderbird as a powerful supernatural being. In many different mythological traditions, birds forge a connection with heaven or the gods.

THE PEREGRINE FALCON is the fastest creature on Earth, reaching speeds of up to 200 miles (320 kilometers) per hour when it dives. Falconers—who carry their birds on leather-gauntleted fists and often outfit them with leather hoods to protect them from outside distractions and to keep them calm—refer to their birds as their partners. They do not consider themselves to be masters of their birds—sometimes they even consider themselves to be their slaves. A falcon's ascent into the sky and the hunt that follows release a burst of adrenaline in the falconer below. As soon as the bird has caught its prey, its handler approaches, carefully removes the booty, and rewards the bird.

The origins of falconry are obscure. It could be that it first developed in Central Asia around 2000 BCE and spread out from there over time, or it could have arisen independently in a number of different locations. The birds themselves are only distantly related to

Friedrich II von Hohenstaufen with a falcon

other birds of prey such as eagles and vultures, and are probably more closely related to parrots. There are about sixty known species, and they are found everywhere in the world except for Antarctica and a few remote islands. By dramatically expanding the falconers' sphere of influence, the birds lift people to heights they cannot reach on their own. Using their birds to hunt other animals means falconers must tame, train, and control them, and falconry arouses an enthusiasm that is difficult to explain. It requires endless patience and care, for the birds must never be punished, and this may be why the most intimate relationships between humans and birds are manifest in the interaction between falconers and their falcons.

Friedrich ii von Hohenstaufen (1194–1250), who was Holy Roman Emperor from 1220 until his death, has gone down in history as one of the world's most famous falconers. The German naturalist Erwin Stresemann went so far as to label him history's first great ornithologist. Friedrich ii wrote a groundbreaking book on birds in general and falcons in particular: *De arte venandi cum avibus* (published in English in 1943 as *The Art of Falconry by Frederick ii of Hohenstaufen*). The book was based on the multilingual emperor's personal experiences and reflected his intense interest in the anatomy and habits of birds. It covered such subjects as food choices, behavior at different times of day, migration, plumage, and different styles of flight. Friedrich learned how to hunt with falcons in his earliest years, and he combined the crusade of 1228–29 with increasing his knowledge of falconry in the Middle East. At his court, he maintained no fewer than fifty falconers who flew a variety of birds of prey, some of which he received as presents from rulers in northern Europe and Greenland.

The noble classes in medieval times were particularly obsessed with falconry, and hunting with falcons was widespread in the ruling houses of Europe. The Castilian statesman Pero López de Ayala (1332–1407) wrote from his Portuguese prison cell in 1385 that the falcon was "the most noble and best of the raptors, lord and prince of the birds of prey." In 1236, Norway gave King Henry III of England ten gray and three white gyrfalcons. The Sardinian regent Eleonora of Arborea (1347–1404) issued a law protecting falcons on her island. Amazingly enough, the falcon she protected, which is native to many islands in the Mediterranean, was not described for science until 1839, by which time the law had been in effect for more than four hundred years. The name given to the bird, Eleonora's falcon, honors that great fourteenth-century bird enthusiast. Her law made her one of the first bird conservationists in history, even though its intent, of course, was to safeguard falconry as a sport for the nobility. Elizabeth I of England (1533–1603) was also said to be gripped by this obsession. And Louis XIII of France (1601–43) supposedly often hunted bats with peregrine falcons at dusk. (Thanks to the acuity of their eyesight, falcons, unlike humans, can see at dusk as well as they can during the day.) In 1930, a British falconer named Colonel Gilbert Blaine (1874–1955) went so far as to say that there must be an inherited human instinct that accounts for the enormous fascination with the sport.

Which raises the question, is this specialized interaction with falcons a sport, an art, a vocation, or all of the above? Perhaps it is simply the most poetic way people have found to work with birds. With the increasing popularity of firearms toward the latter part of the seventeenth century, hunting with falcons came to an abrupt end—albeit with a few exceptions. The British Falconers' Club, established in 1927, exists to this day, and in northern India and the Middle East, falconry continues to be treasured by the wealthy as a precious ritual. Falcons ensured the survival of Bedouins for a long time, and in the Gulf States, falconry is still an integral part of Bedouin culture. There are said to be more than twenty thousand of these birds of prey in the United Arab Emirates alone. To ensure that the birds can travel freely with their owners, passports

Falconers in Abu Dhabi

are drawn up for them, airplane seats are booked for them, and they are ceremoniously settled next to their sheiks in business class. They are treated like family members—like an extra child—and a few years ago, UNESCO recognized falconry as an intangible cultural heritage worthy of protection and promotion. In Abu Dhabi, a German veterinarian named Margit Müller now runs the largest falcon clinic in the world. It was her great fascination with birds of prey that drew her to the job. In a culture where men usually dominate, she has been able to win the complete trust of the sheiks, thanks to her competence, and they now trust her with birds with all manner of problems.

FIFTEEN HUNDRED YEARS before Friedrich II, Aristotle (384–322 BCE) made birds objects of serious study. He examined nests, watched migrating birds fly off, and wondered what molting was really all about. On these subjects, Aristotle was far from infallible, and he borrowed some of his ideas from the realm of fancy rather than fact. For example, he mentioned that some birds apparently hibernated. Given what he knew, this seemed the best explanation for why he never saw certain kinds of birds in winter. (I would add— just as an aside—that the common poorwill, a nocturnal nightjar that lives in the American West, sometimes does enter into a months-long state of torpor.) Aristotle also championed the concept of transmutation, believing that birds can change from one species into another. For example, he believed that summer redstarts turned into robins in the winter. He also advanced the (incorrect) hypothesis that birds do not have kidneys and do not produce urine because any excess fluid in their system is directed to the formation of feathers.

In total, Aristotle mentioned 140 species of birds, although, of course, his selection was restricted to the Mediterranean region. He was also the first person to describe the unusual habits of the cuckoo, which, instead of building a nest of its own, lays its eggs in the nests of other birds. Once its solitary chick hatches, it tips its step-parents' brood out over the edge of the nest, one by one. Despite the fact that Aristotle could not have had any idea about the annual migration of birds to Africa and despite his belief in transmutation, he had his doubts about whether cuckoos turned themselves into birds of prey for the winter. (Although the idea is not so far-fetched when you consider that the cuckoo does bear a slight resemblance to a sparrowhawk, an adaptation that gives it time to lay its egg after scaring away the owners of the nest it has targeted.)

Many writings are attributed to Aristotle, although it is not always clear if he actually wrote them. For example, later historians credited him with dividing birds into those that lived on land and those that lived in rivers, lakes, or on the ocean. He categorized them according to whether they had hooked talons, or whether they ate worms, thistles, or wood beetles, or whether they were dovelike or heavy bodied, or split- or web-footed—divisions we would consider today as hairsplitting.

BY THE EARLY Middle Ages, Aristotle's writings on natural history had sunk into oblivion, and for a long time, religious interpretations, dubious observations, and superstition regained the upper hand. There surely must have been people here and there who continued to be tremendously interested in birds, but traces of their interest are hard to find. The learned abbess Hildegard von Bingen (1098–1179) comes to mind. In her book *Physica*, she writes about fifty species of birds, using the classical elements of earth, water, and air to separate them into "hot," "warm," or "cold." The book is basically a compilation of folk remedies of her time. In it, she describes the effects birds have on people and which birds people should or should not eat. Perhaps we should not judge her too harshly for having no qualms about including flies, bees, cicadas, grasshoppers, wasps, fireflies, and bats in the same category as birds. She was probably largely self-taught and relied on direct observation, although she must have had some contact with trappers and hunters from time to time. It is not too much of a stretch to believe that vultures still lived along the Rhine in her day, but what are the chances that she ever saw an ostrich or a parrot?

OTHERS GRADUALLY BEGAN to separate mythology and folklore from empirical evidence, but is there someone who might be thought of as the first "real" ornithologist? The answer differs depending on which country you are talking about, who you ask, and, to a certain extent, which epoch you are referring to. Ornithology first became established as a science in the nineteenth century, but before that, there were a number of naturalists and scientists who devoted themselves primarily or exclusively to birds—although it has to be said that there was often little correlation between the intensity of their devotion and the value of their observations to science.

While he was a student at Cambridge, an Englishman named William Turner (probably 1508–68) discovered the unique and somewhat sinister marshlands of East Anglia known as the fens. At the time, they were still home to numerous cranes and black terns, which unfortunately disappeared as the fens were drained—a project that began in earnest in the 1630s. Turner was a committed Nonconformist and had to flee to Continental Europe to avoid religious persecution. He spent many years in Italy, where he earned a degree in medicine. In 1544, in Cologne, he published his major work, *Avium praecipuarum historia* (which appeared in English in 1903 with the title *Turner on Birds*), which he dedicated to the young Prince of Wales. It is one of the earliest books on birds and contains descriptions of 130 different species. While traveling in Switzerland, he struck up a friendship with the Swiss naturalist Conrad Gessner. After Henry VIII's death, he returned briefly to England before having to leave again temporarily when the strict Catholic Mary I ("Bloody Mary") ascended to the throne.

In the course of his life, Gessner (1516–65) studied many different animals. He devoted a whole volume of his encyclopedic work *Historiae animalium* (A History of Animals) to birds. It was published in 1555 with simple yet eye-catching woodcuts to illustrate the 217 entries. Many later critics view Gessner's work as a compilation of stories rather than as science, but it is unfair to judge him outside the context of his times, and he can be credited with creating the first zoological work in the modern sense, combining ancient, medieval, and modern knowledge.

Ulisse Aldrovandi (1522–1605) was a professor of philosophy in Bologna. With *Ornithologiae* (Ornithology), he created a book similar to Gessner's that offered high-quality illustrations and detailed anatomical descriptions. Aldrovandi, who also spent a lot of time studying dragons, was criticized for mixing fantastical creatures in with real birds, although some of the birds he saw when he visited the Medici aviaries in Florence—where he wondered at the sight of such birds as helmeted and great curassows, red cardinals, village indigobirds, pin-tailed whydahs, turkeys, pheasants, and peacocks—must have looked pretty fantastical to him. Aldrovandi's cabinet of curiosities—a display of extraordinary objects that celebrated the marvels of the natural world—is said to have contained more than eight thousand objects.

The Englishman John Ray (1627–1705) is often counted among the forerunners of modern ornithologists. Despite being the son of a blacksmith, he studied at Cambridge. He was among those who worked hard to replace the fabulous accounts of Aristotle and the Middle Ages with scientific facts. He is also considered to be the father of British botany. He wrote a book about the flora of Cambridgeshire, but his most important contribution to natural history was *The Ornithology of Francis Willughby. Translated and enlarged with many additions etc. by John Ray.*

Ray became friends with Francis Willughby (1635–72) when the two were at university together. They first toured the coast of Great Britain researching gulls before embarking on a three-year journey across mainland Europe, where they became acquainted with, and dissected, numerous birds that were as yet unknown in their homeland. Interestingly enough, they found many of these birds at markets, where bird catchers were offering them for sale. They were interested not only in the birds' anatomy, but also in the parasites they carried. In the book, Ray documented his many years of working with Willughby, who contributed to the text but died before the book was published. Willughby not only financed their journeys, he also left his friend a generous pension, and Ray looked after Willughby's children after his death. The book was issued in numerous editions, each with newly prepared illustrations. It embodied the final attempt to document everything that was known about birds in a single work, and from this point on, bats were no longer counted as birds. Finally, ornithology was entering the realm of science.

{ 2 }

Bedazzlement

W HEN THE FIRST birds of paradise arrived with Ferdinand
Magellan's ship *Victoria* in Seville harbor on September 8,
1522, along with a priceless cargo of spices, they looked nothing
like their living counterparts. The specimens did not come close to
conveying the living birds' fascinating splendor. They were gossamer-
light, dried skins wrapped around a stick. Nothing remained but
long silky feathers, glossy and shimmering with color. Antonio
Pigafetta (1491–1534), who traveled on another of the ships in Magellan's fleet to document the journey around the world, wrote:

> *These birds are as large as thrushes; they have small heads, long*
> *beaks, legs slender like a writing pen, and a span in length; they have*
> *no wings, but instead of them long feathers of different colours, like*
> *plumes: their tail is like that of the thrush. All the feathers, except*
> *those of the wings, are of a dark colour; they never fly, except when*
> *the wind blows. They told us that these birds come from the terrestrial*
> *Paradise, and they call them "bolon dinata" that is divine birds.*

Juan Sebastián Elcano, the captain of the *Victoria,* received the first specimens from the sultan of Bacan as a gift. When the natural historian Francisco López de Gómara examined them, he declared, "We are of the opinion that these birds are nourished by dew and the nectar of spice trees. Whether that is true or not, one thing is certain, they never decay."

The birds were said to come from islands in the vicinity of *terra australis incognita* (the unknown land of the south). Their provenance was only the beginning of a legend that would continue to grow over the centuries and came close to causing strife between the colonial powers of the day. Probably it was the incompleteness and mysteriousness of the birds' remains that gave rise to their distinctive mystique. They were exotic treasures and objects of desire.

What no one wanted to believe, even though Pigafetta had hinted at the practice, was that while preserving the skins, the islanders removed not only the flesh and bones but also the feet and sometimes even the wings. The skins' amazed recipients took that as proof that the birds never touched the ground but spent their lives floating on the breeze, and that they therefore deserved to be classified in their own separate order. Following this line of reasoning, one Bishop Simolus wrote in 1597:

> *As long as they live, they live the lives of angels, but when they die, they fall from the sky like the Devil, never to return. And so they are a symbol for sinners who, suddenly cast from God's grace, tumble down into Hell.*

Carolus Clusius (1526–1609) was a naturalist who worked at the court of the Holy Roman Emperor Rudolf II of the House of Habsburg and then, starting in 1593, as a professor at the University of Leiden. He is credited with naming new species, including the greater bird of paradise and the king bird of paradise. Even though he, too, had never seen a live bird of paradise, he saw through the taxidermists' mutilations, but nobody wanted to listen to him because that would have disturbed not only the birds' mystical aura but also commercial interests and relationships. And so the mystique of the divine birds continued for quite some time. Two esteemed ornithologists, Carl Linnaeus (1707–78) and George-Louis Leclerc de Buffon (1707–88), were among those who fell for the fairytale. Linnaeus even came up with a name for them: *Paradisea apoda* or "footless bird of paradise."

Depictions of the birds in contemporary sketches and watercolors were also far from realistic, as belief in the birds' miraculous qualities was too strong for obvious but mundane facts to prevail, and artists were handicapped because they could not observe live birds in their natural surroundings. In his book *Ornithologiae,* Aldrovandi depicted the bird without legs and even surmised that the two long tail feathers served in lieu of feet. It was not until the middle of the seventeenth century that it was finally demonstrated that the birds did, indeed, have legs, feet, and wings.

A FRENCH SHIP'S surgeon named René Primevère Lesson (1794–1849) started out on the trail of birds, butterflies, and plants in his youth, and when he arrived in New Guinea in 1823–24, he wrote enthusiastically:

> *We were walking carefully following paths made by wild pigs in the shady depths of the thick forest around the port of Doréy, when a tiny emerald-green bird of paradise flew over our heads with airy swoops, graceful and agile. To us it seemed like a meteor, its fiery tail splitting the air with a long trail of light.*

Lesson must have been one of the very first Western naturalists to see a live specimen of this bird. He published the results of his research in 1835 under the title *Histoire naturelle des oiseaux de paradis* (The Natural History of Birds of Paradise). These rare and seemingly mysterious creatures could put bird hunters into a state of high excitement until well into the second half of the nineteenth century. In 1872, the Italian naturalist Luigi d'Albertis (1841–1901) traveled around New Guinea. Plagued by dropsy, he dragged himself through the jungle on painfully swollen legs and feet, but he forgot all about his discomfort the moment he set eyes on a bird of paradise: "My excitement was so great that when I saw it fall I ran to secure it, forgetting the state of my legs, though a moment before I had hardly been able to drag them along."

The days when gorgeous bird of paradise feathers decorated hats in fashionable circles are now long gone, but the residents of

Papua New Guinea have used the birds' plumage to decorate elaborate headdresses worn on ceremonial occasions, primarily by men, since time immemorial and continue to do so. In addition, feathers and skins were traditionally valued as trade items. Laws today try to balance respect for cultural practices with the urgent need for conservation of these beautiful birds with their spectacular, showy plumes.

Ornithologists are still on the trail of birds of paradise in the jungles of Papua New Guinea; however, their goals are completely different from those of bird hunters a couple of centuries ago. Jack Dumbacher, the curator of the California Academy of Sciences, is one of these ornithologists. His specialties are the ecology and evolution of birds of paradise and tropical diseases in this part of the world. He says that working in New Guinea is like going back in time. Incidentally, Dumbacher made a splash in ornithological circles when he discovered that the poison homobatrachotoxin can be found hiding in the skin and feathers of the orange-and-black hooded pitohui, a kind of oriole. This pitohui is one of the few poisonous birds in the world, as Dumbacher discovered when he accidently trapped one in a net set for birds of paradise and the pitohui scratched him as he removed it. As he was sucking the wound, he realized that his mouth had gone numb. At first, he thought nothing of it. It was only a year later, when he absentmindedly put one of the bird's feathers into his mouth and immediately noticed its extremely unpleasant taste, that he thought to research the subject further. Homobatrachotoxin is more toxic than strychnine and comes from a particular kind of beetle the pitohui eats.

THE CONQUERORS OF the New World hunted other airborne treasures. Some—minuscule winged jewels that buzzed around their heads in tiny clouds—were particularly perplexing. Were these creatures insects or birds? The French called them *oiseaux*

mouches (bird flies), the Portuguese *beija-flores* (flower kissers) or *chupa-flores* (flower suckers), the Spanish *picaflores* (flower stingers). The English called them *humbirds* from about 1640 and later changed their name to hummingbird. Very tiny species in Brazil were also called *besourinhos* (little beetles), and the Cubans gave the bee hummingbird the enchanting name *zunzuncito*. The German name, *Kolibri*—also used in Spanish today (*colibrí*)—is likely Caribbean in origin. In 1758, Carl Linnaeus, who knew 18 of the 340 species known today, gave it the scientific name *Trochilus*.

The first mention of this frenetically active little bird can be found in the travel journals of Jean de Léry (1536–1613), who belonged to a crew of mariners sent to the Brazilian coast. In his journal, published in 1557, he mentioned a bird whose body was "no larger than that of a hornet or a stag beetle." He called it "an extraordinary wonder and a masterpiece of minuteness." Georg Markgraf

(1610–48), who traveled to Brazil in 1638, wrote in his book *Historia naturalis Brasiliae* (A Natural History of Brazil), published in 1648, that the ruby-throated hummingbird, weighing in at slightly over one-tenth of an ounce (barely 4 grams), was the most beautiful of all the hummingbirds, and he had seen many on his travels.

Acrobats of the air, hummingbirds can quickly make themselves scarce when danger threatens. But they can also be fearless, as many observers have noted with some amazement.

> *See it darting through the air almost as quick as thought!—now it is within a yard of your face!—in an instant gone!—now it flutters from flower to flower to sip the silver dew—it is now a ruby—now a topaz—now an emerald—now all burnished gold!*

So wrote the English naturalist Charles Waterton (1782–1865) after traveling through Latin America in the early nineteenth century.

After birds of paradise, hummingbirds were among the highlights of eighteenth- and nineteenth-century natural history collections. In many parts of the world, bird catchers sold their hastily preserved plunder to natural history museums and bird lovers. In Victorian drawing rooms, they served the same purpose as decorative flowers—and often ended up as dust collectors.

After traveling to South America and other lands on the corvette *La Coquille*, Lesson described nearly forty new species and produced a multivolume monograph with 261 wonderfully detailed and hand-colored lithographs. The English naturalist Philip Henry Gosse (1810–88)—perhaps best known for popularizing the home aquarium—made detailed observations of hummingbirds in Jamaica and relied on Lesson's work to identify them. He also took it upon himself to denounce the widely held misconception that hummingbirds could be dangerous to people. He wrote in *The Birds of Jamaica* that "the spirit of curiosity is manifested by this little bird… stories of Humming-birds attacking men, and striking at the eyes with their needle-like bills, originated, I have no doubt, in the exaggeration of fear, misinterpreting this innocent curiosity."

It is no accident that you almost only see hummingbirds in flight, for, more than any other land-based bird, they have freed themselves from the shackles of the Earth. They cannot even walk.

Hummingbirds are primarily (although not exclusively) nectar feeders, and the reciprocal affinity between hummingbirds and flowers was long described as "love," because people did not understand the concept of a close symbiotic relationship and had no idea that birds and plants could evolve together. Many species of birds visit flowers, but none is as exquisitely adapted for the task as hummingbirds. Not only because the length and curve of their beaks fit the forms of the flowers they visit (sunbirds, for example, share this characteristic), but also because of the unique way they approach flowers. Whereas most birds need to perch next to blooms, this is not the case for most hummingbirds. You could say they "stand" suspended in the air in front of flowers while feeding. Gosse did notice, however, that streamertails (a species of hummingbird found in Jamaica) are not always airborne when they feed.

> They do not invariably probe flowers upon the wing; one may frequently observe them thus engaged, when alighted and sitting with closed wings, and often they partially sustain themselves by clinging with the feet to a leaf while sucking, the wings being expanded, and vibrating.

And, it should be added, hummingbirds, like insects, also pollinate flowers while they are snacking on nectar.

By the middle of the seventeenth century, people knew that hummingbirds drank nectar, and a couple of decades later they observed

that they ate insects as well, for they need not only carbohydrates but also protein and fat to survive. However, it took a very long time for this to become common knowledge, partly because it contradicted the much-loved romantic notion that these wonderful birds sustained themselves on nothing but drops of dew, air, and love. You could fill a whole book with descriptions of experiments in hummingbird nutrition. In 1837, the German biologist Lorenz Oken (1779–1851) knew that they could survive no more than a couple of months on "sweet plant juices" alone but as long as a year "if they are free to fly in a room with only canvas covering the windows so flies can get in." Many different people tried hard to introduce hummingbirds to Europe, but it soon became clear that they could not survive there—and most did not even survive the journey over.

It can be exhausting to watch hummingbirds darting about. How is it possible to understand a creature whose movements are so fast that we cannot observe them with the senses Nature gave us? Toward the end of the nineteenth century, observers could capture the flight of other birds on film and break the sequence down into individual frames. The high frequency of the hummingbird's wing beat (which, as we now know, is from 12 to 80 strokes per second depending on the species) called for other methods. In 1928, MIT professor Harold E. Edgerton (1903–90)—who would later shoot the famous photograph of the impact of a single drop landing in a bowl of milk—combined a strobe light with a film camera in a friend's garden to film hummingbirds comfortable around people. He was soon able to film at a rate of 540 frames per second. Edgerton provided proof that hummingbirds beat their wings horizontally and can fly backwards. He also discovered that when they hover, they rotate their wings, and as they power them backward, they displace air. You could compare how they move their wings to how swimmers move their arms when they are doing the backstroke. Nature's wonders indeed.

3

Strutting Someone Else's Stuff

E RWIN STRESEMANN WAS in charge of the Department of Ornithology at the Zoological Museum at the University of Berlin from 1921 to 1961. In his history of ornithology, he gives a detailed description of the squabbling that took place in the seventeenth and eighteenth centuries over the nomenclature and classification of animals. At that time, the question was whether to use the binomial system proposed by Linnaeus or the behaviorally based approach of Buffon. In the days before the two approaches were combined into a single system, scientists were in a difficult position: naturalists were setting out to comb the world for its treasures, and when previously unknown animals were discovered, they needed to be named and assigned their places in a system of classification that was still under construction.

Initially, most of these costly expeditions were undertaken by the French, who hoped to profit from them financially and otherwise. In 1765, the British and Russians decided to join in. Catherine the

Great invited researchers, including Swedes and Germans, to the Russian Academy of Sciences. Her plan was to dispatch those who accepted her invitation on voyages of discovery throughout her far-flung realm.

The plants and animals brought back by the expeditions were soon put on display in a variety of settings. Take, for example, the installations at the London home of the wealthy English collector Ashton Lever (1729–88). In 1784, the Museum Leverianum housed no fewer than 28,000 objects or, more accurately, exhibits. In a circular room lit by a skylight, there were a couple of hundred stuffed birds labeled according to the Linnaean system. The exhibits included such rarities as the Mascarene parrot and the white gallinule, both of which became extinct in the nineteenth century. A few decades later, however, the public lost interest, and the most noteworthy specimens were sold to the natural history collection at the imperial court in Vienna, the forerunner of the current Vienna Museum of Natural History.

The noted French ornithologist François Levaillant (1753–1824) focused exclusively on birds early on in his life. He spent his first decade in Surinam—where his wealthy father was the French consul—accompanying his parents on their rambles through the primeval forests. He soon began shooting birds with a blowpipe and creating his own small collection. He returned to France with his family in 1763 and subsequently studied natural history there. In 1781, the Dutchman Conrad Jacob Temminck sponsored Levaillant on an expedition to South Africa. Levaillant returned after more than three years with an impressive collection of more than two thousand bird skins. He was disappointed to find that no scholars in Paris were interested in his specimens, partly because not a single one understood what they were now that the great Buffon had retired from public life. Luckily, he finally found a few well-disposed and wealthy bird lovers in the Netherlands.

Levaillant wanted to write a book, and he attracted the support of Casimir Varon, a literary man who was gifted with a vivid imagination and knew how to embellish facts to suit public taste. This involved exaggerating Levaillant's experiences and going so far as to invent a journey from Orange Free State (an independent republic in southern Africa controlled by the Dutch East India Company) to the Tropic of Capricorn. In the resulting opus, *Travels into the interior parts of Africa, by way of the Cape of Good Hope; in the years 1780, 1781, 82, 83, 84, and 85,* the length of his travels was also considerably increased.

Levaillant followed Buffon's descriptive naming system and often gave the birds he discovered very simple names, some of which mimicked the sounds they made, such as *brubru* or *boubou*. He was briefly imprisoned during the French Revolution, but was freed after Robespierre was executed in 1794. The naturalist was not shy about adding other people's collections of newly discovered exotic birds to his own inventory, including those of French doctor René Geoffroy de Villeneuve, who returned from Senegal in 1795.

Levaillant happily included a mix of his own birds and those appropriated from others in his multivolume work *The Birds of Africa,* which appeared in a number of different editions. After his book was published, Levaillant finally managed to attract the interest of the National Museum of Natural History in Paris, which bought a number of his bird skins. Although this was an era when the collective imagination was downright obsessed with the wonders of Nature and experts were laying the groundwork for scientific ornithology as we know it today, and despite all the excitement about birds, Levaillant died in great poverty in his tiny cottage in La Noue near Sézanne in the Champagne region of France.

Soon after Levaillant's death, other experts began to pick away at his claims to glory. They noticed that in his book *The Natural History of Parrots,* he had taken illustrations from Buffon's

Richard Meinertzhagen showing off a kori bustard, Nairobi 1915

encyclopedic and widely read *Natural History* and altered them so that their origins were not immediately obvious. A Swedish zoologist named Carl Sundevall (1801–75) proved that Levaillant had cobbled together many of his specimens using skins from different birds. Of the 284 African species he described, 10 cannot be classified at all, 71 originated outside the continent, 50 more are suspect, and 10 are constructed from the feathers of different species. That is somewhat surprising given that Levaillant himself had complained about profit-hungry traders who fabricated fraudulent specimens. Even though it is difficult to separate fact from fiction in Levaillant's work, Erwin Stresemann did not think that his reputation was in serious danger.

> *Even today only an expert can distinguish true from false in the cleverly concocted brew that Levaillant served up to his readers. But there is always enough useful material left to vindicate L's original reputation. He was really an excellent observer of birds and knowledgeable understanding [sic] of their behavior, and in fact gifted as few others have been in communicating his idea not only vividly but attractively.*

THE THREAD OF deception is woven into ornithological history, revealing itself in ever-changing patterns whenever it is exposed. Politics and ornithology came together in a remarkably tightly knit and mutually beneficial relationship in the life of the aristocrat Richard Meinertzhagen (1878–1967). There is no doubt that he is one of the most brilliant and mysterious figures ever to have stepped into the ornithological limelight. The son of a banker of German ancestry, he grew up in late Victorian times in the upper echelons of colonial British society. Early on in his career, he accompanied Herbert Spencer—famous among other things for coining the phrase "survival of the fittest"—on field trips. He was the author of numerous scholarly publications, and he was born early enough to know Charles Darwin personally. He even sat on Darwin's knee.

Meinertzhagen was educated in England and Germany. Shortly before the end of the nineteenth century, he became a career officer in the British army and was posted to places such as India, Burma, East Africa, Palestine, and Syria. Meinertzhagen experienced and had a hand in the outcome of many decisive historical conflicts, some of them in the company of T.E. Lawrence (Lawrence of Arabia). In Palestine, he was Chief Political Officer for Sir Edmund Allenby, commander of the British forces, and was involved in the 1917 victory over the Turkish army. At the Paris Peace Conference in 1919, he served as military advisor to the British delegation. Although he officially resigned his commission in 1925, he maintained a connection to the military; he was even mobilized during World War II and wounded at Dunkirk. There is some speculation that he was working as a spy during these decades. Besides that, Meinertzhagen was known for his extremely active imagination, going so far as to describe an imaginary meeting with Adolph Hitler in his diary.

Meinertzhagen's particular areas of interest were bird migration and the intriguing plumage patterns of desert birds. When he was stationed in Palestine during World War I, under Allenby's command, he used the theodolites (rotating telescopes that measure horizontal and vertical angles) at two anti-aircraft gun stations that were connected by telephone to calculate the speed and altitude of birds in flight. He was also the proud possessor of a comprehensive collection of 600,000 bird lice. He was chairman of the British Ornithologists' Club, wrote books about the birds of Egypt and Arabia, and sometimes traveled on behalf of the avid collector Lord Walter Rothschild, whose own story is covered later in this book. Meinertzhagen had 25,000 bird skins in his collection, which was purchased by the Natural History Museum in London in 1954.

Athene blewitti or forest owlet

Supposedly, he bagged half the birds in his collection himself, and rumor has it that he always carried a tiny pistol in his walking stick in order to circumvent occasional bans on shooting.

It could be that Meinertzhagen cultivated his interest in birds and bird lice just so he had an alibi. We may never know for certain. The authors of the first three biographies to appear after his death could not find any reason to seriously doubt his integrity. It was only thirty years later, when an ornithologist named Pamela Rasmussen was investigating the birds of India for a book and inspected the bird skins that Meinertzhagen had collected in his free time as an officer in the colonial army, that he began to appear in an unfavorable light. Rasmussen had come across some specimens that looked suspicious. Things began to snowball after the publication of an article in *Ibis*, the journal of the British Ornithologists' Union, in which the respected Irish researcher Alan Knox proved that some of Meinertzhagen's skins were incorrectly labeled. In the case of two skins, Knox suspected that Meinertzhagen hadn't bagged the birds himself in France but had pilfered the skins from the Natural History Museum in London, and that they were also much older than the dates recorded on the new labels he had given them. This case concerned a relatively common bird, a common redpoll. This, in turn, fueled Rasmussen's suspicions. Perhaps Meinertzhagen had done the same thing with birds that were much harder to find?

Rasmussen traveled to Tring, an ornithological mecca 30 miles (50 kilometers) northwest of London where Meinertzhagen's skins are now stored. She took them out of their acid-free cardboard boxes and looked at them more closely under a microscope to find out what methods had been used to preserve them. The detective work included taking x-rays of the skins. As soon as a suspicious skin was found, it was checked against the Natural History Museum's collection to find out if it was missing. In the case of the forest owlet *(Athene blewitti)*, which is considered to be one of the rarest birds in India, researchers established that Meinertzhagen's skin had been worked on to obscure its original source. He claimed to have bagged the bird in October 1914 in Mandvi, but thanks to a small speck of yellow cotton that he had obviously overlooked, it could finally be proven that it had been shot by an army officer named James Davidson in 1884—at a location nearly 200 miles

(320 kilometers) from the one Meinertzhagen had specified. More specimens were found with such scraps of material in them, and the researchers proved that the labels on fourteen species had been falsified.

Meinertzhagen is regarded as the perpetrator of "the greatest ornithological fraud ever committed—a convoluted skein of theft and data falsification," as journalist John Seabrook described it. The British ornithologist Tim Birkhead has nothing nice to say about him either, going even further and painting him as a "pathological liar and self-promoter." In his 2008 book *The Meinertzhagen Mystery*, biographer Brian Garfield also voiced the grave suspicion that Meinertzhagen's wife, Ann "Annie" Jackson (1888–1928)—an ornithologist who first recognized that common redshanks born in Iceland visit the British Isles—did not accidently shoot herself in the head while handling a revolver (which is how the official version goes), but was murdered by Meinertzhagen—horribly enough, just a few months after the birth of their third child. Garfield bases his suspicion on inconsistencies in descriptions of events surrounding her death. If it really was murder, it was probably motivated not only by the fact that he wanted to leave her for another woman but also by the fact that his wife knew of his deception and if she had made it known, Meinertzhagen's reputation as an ornithologist would have been seriously damaged.

4

Laying the Groundwork for Science

A S THE EIGHTEENTH century rolled over into the nineteenth, the impact of colonizing North America spread into the spheres of natural history and ornithology. Bird watchers came to explore the continent or combined the business of settlement with pleasure. They wanted not only to discover the animals of the New World but also to introduce them to the nature-loving public on both sides of the Atlantic.

Mark Catesby (1683–1749) was the first to write about the birds (and other animals) in North America, and he filled his books with magnificent illustrations. However, there is no doubt that Alexander Wilson (1766–1813) was the more important figure as far as the science of ornithology is concerned. Wilson's roots lay in Scotland. The son of a weaver, he made his living weaving and selling silks, muslins, and ribbons until his criticisms of social inequality in Scotland landed him in serious trouble with the law, even getting him arrested a number of times. Finally, in anticipation of an unfair trial in May 1794, he boarded a ship bound for the United States.

Wilson ended up in Philadelphia, where he worked as a teacher. It was a stroke of luck that the area was the perfect place from which to observe bird migration, for he had been interested in birds before leaving Europe. When the self-taught Wilson met the naturalist William Bartram, the idea was born for a series of books entitled *American Ornithology*. Over time, Wilson documented the vast majority of North American birds in what was then a most unusual fashion. He didn't just draw them after they had been shot. Instead, he immersed himself in their natural surroundings while he traveled across the country—on foot, on horseback, or by ship—observing live birds caged or flying free. As he did so, he evolved a completely new way of capturing birds' likenesses, both in approach and in content. His work not only proved that the birds in North America were just as impressive as those in Europe, but also revolutionized wildlife illustration. On top of all this, he promoted himself as a patriotic American. It is therefore little wonder that then-president Thomas Jefferson—whom Wilson had confidently called upon at the White House to interest him in a subscription to his work—was quickly persuaded to sign up. Tragically, although he had devoted most of his life to producing his book, Wilson did not live to see publication of the final volumes.

NEITHER DID WILSON live to see that his work would one day be closely associated with the work of the "Prince of Musignan," better known as Charles Lucien Bonaparte (1803–57). Charles was the nephew of Napoleon Bonaparte, who lost no time disinheriting his brother Lucien when he married Alexandrine de Bleschamps, because he could not forgive his renegade sibling for marrying someone he considered to be socially inferior. The young Charles Lucien grew up in Italy and was made a prince by grace of the Pope. When he married his cousin Zénaïde, he received a generous dowry from his father-in-law, Joseph Bonaparte, the former king of Naples

Flamingo by Mark Catesby

Charles Lucien Bonaparte

and Spain. In 1822, the couple immigrated to the United States and settled near Philadelphia. During the ocean voyage, Bonaparte observed storm-petrels and even managed to shoot a few. In his new country, the talkative, diminutive, stocky Bonaparte (who looked amazingly like Napoleon) became a member of the Academy of Natural Sciences and soon set about studying the birds of North America (in libraries, not in the field, alas), expanding the volumes written by Alexander Wilson, who had died a decade before, and publishing the revised series from 1825 to 1833 under the title *American Ornithology, or the Natural History of Birds Inhabiting the United States, not Given by Wilson.* Bonaparte found the ornithological collection at the Academy of Natural Sciences of Philadelphia, which had recently been updated with specimens collected by a Major Long in the Rocky Mountains, most useful.

The continued westward advance of the settlement frontier was one of the main reasons Wilson's work needed to be updated. Another was that certain facts had to be corrected. Bonaparte owned a long-eared owl from Madagascar and had observed how its plumage changed over its lifetime. This first-hand knowledge helped him catch some of Wilson's mistakes. For example, Wilson had often been unaware of the differences in plumage between males, females, and juveniles, sometimes attributing each to completely different species. While Bonaparte was making his changes, he was being observed suspiciously by people extraordinarily worried about Wilson's reputation, which is understandable when you consider that natural history in those days was not an obscure field of study with a limited audience but the most important area of scientific inquiry in America.

A few years later, in 1828, before the final volume in the series was published, financial circumstances forced Bonaparte to return to Europe. For the next two decades, he resided in Rome, using the city as a base from which to explore the fauna of the Italian peninsula. However, he had little time for field trips after he became politically active and assumed the position of vice president in the legislature. In this role, he signed a declaration that called the people of Rome to arms. When the French army conquered Rome to reinstate the sovereignty of the Pope, Bonaparte left first for Marseilles, then for Paris, London, and Leiden, where he spent a year and had his hands full with the twelve thousand birds in the museum there. Unfortunately, he did not have the benefit of his reference library, because he had been forced to leave his precious books in Rome. It was Bonaparte who gave the distinctive blue-headed Wilson's bird of paradise (whose common name already honored Wilson) the Latin name *Diphyllodes respublica* (known today as *Cicinnurus respublica*), putting on record his republican sympathies and his deep contempt for the uncle who had disowned

his family. By this time, the scholarly world had acknowledged Bonaparte as one of the world's leading experts on birds.

In 1850, Bonaparte received permission from his cousin, and president at the time, Napoleon III to return to France and he lived out the rest of his life in Paris. "In the French metropolis, he is now the leader, supporter, and protector of all the foreign naturalists he welcomes into his hospitable home," wrote Baron J.W. von Müller, who was hard at work on his own books about birds in Africa. John Gould was one of the ornithologists who met with Bonaparte in Paris. With the financial support of Isidore Geoffroy Saint-Hilaire, Bonaparte then devoted himself to working on the *Conspectus generum avium* (A Catalog of Bird Species) at the National Museum of Natural History in Paris, a work that was supposed to include all the species of birds in the world. In his attempt to document everything that was known and to clear up scientific terminology, Bonaparte drew on the catalogs of many different museums. His first volume appeared in 1850. Despite covering an impressive 1,075 genera, the work was never finished.

JOHN JAMES AUDUBON (1785–1851)—who today is the undisputed icon for bird conservation in North America—is said to have captured the likeness of more than twice as many species of birds as Wilson, which also meant capturing the birds: "I wish I had eight pairs of hands, and another body to shoot the specimens," he wrote. He was born of French parents (his given name was Jean-Jacques) on the island of Hispaniola (now Haiti), but the family soon moved to Brittany in France. Apparently, he preferred roaming the countryside in search of eggs, nests, and flowers to sitting still at a desk in school. At the age of eighteen, he was sent to the United States to manage an estate his father had inherited. In order to avoid compulsory service in Napoleon's army, he made the move to the New World permanent, and he was soon spending a great deal of time sketching birds. When the United States declared war on Great Britain in 1812, he took American citizenship.

Audubon roamed the country and built up his collection of artwork. During one of his excursions, he left two hundred drawings for safekeeping in a wooden chest with a relative. On his return, he discovered that rats had completely shredded his works and used them to make a cozy nest. Despite this setback, he continued to work tirelessly. Unfortunately, his drawings by themselves were not enough to interest influential people in his work, but he couldn't even consider publishing a book without well-to-do subscribers to cover the cost of printing. It didn't help that he was not a scientist or that Charles Lucien Bonaparte was working on a similar project with his follow-up volumes to Wilson's *American Ornithology*. Moreover, his large, detailed watercolors needed an experienced printer to do them justice. In 1826, he set off to France and Britain in search of sponsors, and he eventually found the printer he needed in Edinburgh. Audubon was a talented self-promoter, and his good looks and frontier attire were great assets in his business dealings. To capitalize on his natural assets, he rubbed bear grease into his shoulder-length, chestnut-brown hair until it shone.

Audubon succeeded in breathing more vitality into the birds he drew than any of his predecessors had achieved. His drawings of diving terns, where he captures on paper the speed of their descent through the air, are a good example. Every now and then, he arranged birds in arresting scenes that were not always true to nature in every detail but achieved his goal of catching and holding the viewer's eye. He did have scruples about going out and shooting birds for his work, as the following disturbing story shows. He had purchased a live golden eagle from a trapper. He was used to drawing dead birds, and he found it much more difficult to draw a bird that was alive. Supposedly, he then wrestled with himself for a while, trying to decide whether he should free the bird or kill it as painlessly

John James Audubon

as possible. After he had decided on the latter course of action, he took the bird into a closet and put it under a tent he had fashioned from bedclothes. He then placed a pan of burning charcoal under the tent. Unfortunately, he did not succeed in killing the bird with the suffocating fumes, and in the end, he resorted to stabbing it in the heart. This incident with the poor bird is said to have traumatized Audubon to such an extent that he suffered a heart attack that required the ministrations of no fewer than three doctors.

After Audubon recovered, he traveled by ship to the Florida Keys, the Gulf of Mexico, the coast of Quebec, and the upper reaches of the Missouri River. He never crossed the Continental Divide, and the West Coast birds he drew were specimens sent to him by other bird enthusiasts. His book *The Birds of America* contained 415 large, hand-colored plates depicting 1,065 birds belonging to 491 different species. Three hundred, or possibly only 200, copies were printed, of which there are still about 160 in collections around the world, the remaining copies having been broken down for the color plates. A reprint in a smaller, much more affordable format was enough of a financial success that he could buy a piece of land on the Hudson River in a place called Carmansville, which has since disappeared from the map. Here he built a beautiful timber house,

Great horned owl by
John James Audubon

where, with the help of his sons, he worked for up to fourteen hours a day on three volumes on North American mammals. As his health declined and his eyesight deteriorated, he lost his means of supporting himself. He died at the relatively young age of sixty-five.

WITH THE SELECTION of birds he drew, John Gould (1804–81) extended bird watchers' horizons to all the continents except Africa and Antarctica. Gould was born in southwest England and began blowing out birds' eggs and stuffing animals early in his life. He eventually moved to London, where he worked for a short time as a gardener before setting up shop and making a name for himself as a taxidermist. He then practiced his trade at the museum of the newly founded Zoological Society of London, where he got to know the leading naturalists of the day. Meeting his future wife, Elizabeth, was a piece of good fortune for him, as she possessed just the artistic skill that he lacked. Rumor has it that he did not draw any of the illustrations in his books himself, even though he was credited as being the artist in some of them, while others who should have been credited were overlooked. News of this deceit gradually circulated, leading to his reputation as an unscrupulous profiteer.

The first book he published with his wife was *A Century of Birds from the Himalaya Mountains.* Nicholas Vigors provided the text. The book contained eighty plates showing one hundred birds, and it quickly became a great success, which led to work on other books. Gould was what we would today call a workaholic. Everything around him, including his wife, had to take second place to his entrepreneurial aspirations. Gould helped Darwin identify some of the birds the scientist had brought back from his famous voyage on HMS *Beagle.* In his dealings with Darwin, however, Gould held back from commenting on the scientist's theories to avoid frightening off potential subscribers to his own books, many of whom had religious sensibilities.

Up until that point, Gould's work had been based on skins travelers had brought to him. In 1838, he embarked on a four-month voyage of his own to Tasmania. His wife, who was pregnant with their seventh child at the time, held the fort in Hobart, the capital of the island. At first, Gould depended a great deal on his colleague John Gilbert, until the latter tragically fell victim to an attack by Aborigines on one of their expeditions. Gould then left his pregnant wife to collect birds in Australia, returning to Tasmania for the birth of his son. In 1839, the family traveled together to the area around Sydney, and Gould continued collecting material. After more than two years, the family returned to England, where his wife died a few months later, after giving birth to their eighth child. This was a catastrophe on both a personal and a professional level, for Gould had lost not only his life partner but also a gifted collaborator.

After Elizabeth's death, the artist and lithographer Henry Constantine Richter stepped into her shoes and began to work Gould's rough sketches up into publication-quality illustrations. He did this for eight large-format volumes of *The Birds of Australia and the Adjacent Islands*—which are fascinating to this day for their sumptuous color and scrupulous attention to detail—as well as for *The Birds of Asia* and other titles published by Gould. All told, Richter worked on almost 1,600 color plates. The book on Australia—which, incidentally, had many high-ranking individuals among its subscribers—had 681 hand-colored lithographs and made the bird world of the last of the continents to be discovered accessible to a wider public for the first time. It was also a great success financially.

At the same time as he was busy publishing books, Gould was collecting the skins of more than five thousand hummingbirds. Hummingbirds were his personal specialty, and his prodigious capacity for work was once again evident. With these birds, the particular challenge for his artistic and printing skills was to reproduce the iridescence of the feathers of the male birds as faithfully

Red-tailed comets by John Gould

as possible. Gould's *Monograph of the Trochilidae, or Family of Hummingbirds* appeared in six volumes and one supplement (the first volume came out in 1849) and was another immediate success. Ironically, Gould did not see his first living hummingbird until 1857, when he spied one in Bartram's Garden in Philadelphia, the oldest botanical garden in North America. The way it flew surprised him. He wrote that it "was exactly the opposite of what I had expected." It sounds almost unbelievable, but it seems he had thought hummingbirds moved through the air like butterflies. When he returned to England, he couldn't resist the temptation to bring two hummingbirds back with him in a little cage. He tried to keep them alive with a mixture of sugar, honey, and egg whites. It was common knowledge that it was difficult to feed these tiny creatures, and so it came as no surprise when they died just two days after his arrival in London.

Gould's affair with hummingbirds did not end with the publication of his book. How could he bring more attention to his passion than he already had? In 1851, when the Great Exhibition was being held in the Crystal Palace, he had a pavilion erected not far away on the grounds of the London zoological gardens in Regent's Park with eight rectangular glass cases in which he exhibited to an astounded public 1,500 stuffed specimens of about 320 species of hummingbirds (that would be the vast majority of hummingbirds known today). Almost overnight, this sensational exhibit, which eclipsed most of the bird displays put on by museum ornithologists of the day, made him one of the best-known bird collectors of his time. In the first year alone, he attracted eighty thousand visitors, including Queen Victoria and Prince Albert. In her diary, the queen declared herself enchanted: "It is the most beautiful and complete collection ever seen, and it is impossible to imagine anything so lovely as these little hummingbirds, their variety, and the extraordinary brilliancy of their colours."

Thanks to its great success, the exhibit continued for a second year, and it was with some pride that Gould accepted the title of "the Bird Man" from then on. He wrote about 300 scientific articles, and 377 species of birds are named after him—a record that remains unchallenged to this day. The dazzle faded from the collection, however, as twentieth-century bird watchers and ornithologists began to prize observation of birds in the wild over static public displays. The naturalist W.H. Hudson, who viewed the collection in 1917, acknowledged seeing only bundles of feathers painstakingly held together with wires and accused Gould of being nothing more than a mortician.

WITH THE INVENTION and spread of photography, ornithological artists found themselves in an increasingly precarious position. They had to come up with something special if they were to attract any attention at all. Starting in the 1970s, the Scottish war veteran James "Tim" Westoll (1918–99) gained a certain notoriety among experts when he traveled to many parts of the world in search of interesting birds. At some point, he got it into his head to draw every species of bird and gather them into a single portable volume that could be used as a checklist. He was not entering completely uncharted territory, as others had tried this before. What he was interested in was filling in the gaps others had left. The result of three decades of diligent work was *Birds of the World: The Complete Illustrated Checklist*. In each case, he drew a male and a female, and sometimes a juvenile. He also included about five hundred subspecies. He came up with the idea of including a blue line of varying length at the top of each page to indicate the length of a sparrow compared to the birds in each plate. In total, there were 10,300 birds illustrated in 367 plates. Westoll did not follow the rule that he had to have seen each and every bird with his own eyes. He had actually seen only about one-third of the birds in his book. But still...

{ 5 }

A Bird in the Hand

THE PRACTICE OF keeping birds in captivity has been documented since the time of the Roman Empire. Nightingales and blue rock thrushes (beautifully colored Mediterranean songbirds) were popular as cage-birds. It did not take long for parrots and guinea fowl to be brought back from expeditions to Africa. Magpies were kept in barber shops to entertain clients. And the bones of ravens found during the excavation of Roman towns indicate that they shared people's lives in some way. The Roman senator Lucullus, who lived when today's calendar began, liked to have small birds flying around in his dining room. At his villa in Casinum, the Roman scholar and writer Marcus Terentius Varro had an elaborate enclosure made out of hemp nets strung in a courtyard with colonnaded porticos on three sides and a domed structure at one end, where he is said to have kept many hundreds of birds. Owls were not only prized as decoys to attract unsuspecting songbirds. They were also kept as pets in France, Germany, and Belgium—although this is somewhat surprising given the many demonic associations tied to these fascinating birds. In Italy, *civette,* or more endearingly, *civet-tazze,* as the small owls were called, were especially favored. During the Renaissance, parrots and other exotic birds were particularly popular, and some dealers specialized in trading them. Untold numbers of red-masked goldfinches decorated homes in Europe for at least two thousand years. No one knows who first came up with the idea of training these agile birds to dip a tiny bucket on a chain into a glass to get water to drink, but the activity was described by Pliny in Roman times and was often depicted in paintings in the seventeenth century. Since the ban on wild trapping, these European delights no longer occupy center stage as tame cage-birds and exotic birds have stepped into the limelight.

JOHANN MATTHÄUS BECHSTEIN (1757–1822) was the son of a blacksmith who forged weapons and shod horses. He was supposed to become a clergyman, but he was waylaid by the lure of the woods—a passion that led him to found a school of forestry in Schnepfenthal, Germany. As a teacher, he looked for answers to a multitude of questions about zoology and botany. He gave the barred warbler its beautiful Latin name, *Sylvia nisoria*—"Sylvia" is a woodland sprite and "nisoria" is an old Latin name for the sparrowhawk, which is also barred—and he named the marsh warbler *Acrocephalus palustris.* Whereas other people need quiet in order to work, apparently he needed birdsong in the background to concentrate on anything at all.

Since from my earliest youth I have delighted in being surrounded with birds, [I] am so accustomed to them that I cannot write at my desk with pleasure, or even with attention, unless animated by the warbling of the pleasing little creatures which enliven my room. My passion is carried so far, that I always have about thirty birds around me.

He wrote these words in the preface to his book *The Natural History of Cage Birds,* which was so popular that it went through forty-six editions. Cage-birds, for Bechstein, were "those kept by amateurs, for amusement, in their apartments." Their owners simply did not want to do without the "sweetness of [their] song" or "the beauty of [their] plumage."

His book provides an overview of the species that were available in Central Europe at the time and were considered suitable companions for people. The Dutch were particularly known for keeping birds from foreign lands in large aviaries, but Bechstein, a German, included exotic species such as macaws, canaries, and the so-called Angola finch, which, he explains, "in form and habits, very much resembles our redpole," indicating that Germans must have had some interest in them as well. Most of the birds Bechstein wrote about, however, came from native climes. He said of the barn owl: "They are handsome birds but they make a wretched noise." And he gave this warning about the jackdaw: "When in winter it eats wild garlic in the fields, it smells very strongly of it, and does not lose the scent till it has been a week in the house." He recommended the magpie as the easiest bird to tame. He had handy tips for every potential pet, including the fact that if you kept an oriole, you should not smoke tobacco in the room or the bird would lose the gold color from its plumage.

KEEPING AND RAISING birds first became a form of mass entertainment in the second half of the nineteenth century. Armed with

his father's double-barreled shotgun, Karl Russ (1833–99) was still a schoolboy when he set out to hunt crows. He was a man of great enthusiasms. First, he became an apothecary like his father, and then he turned his hand to writing. He wrote articles on nature and, using his pharmacological knowledge, made a name for himself in advice columns as "a favorite with educated women." In 1872, he founded the magazine *The Feathered World*. He penned many books that were circulated in revised editions for decades, including the encyclopedic *Foreign Aviary Birds*, in which the budgerigar—a bird originally found only in the Australian bush—played an especially prominent role. Whether he was describing the "wedding celebrations" of sparrows and their "quadrilles of love" before they started their next brood, or the cranes that returned to the roofs of people's homes like "family friends," he embraced the kind of anthropomorphism that was typical in popular writing of his day.

Russ's striking innovation was the idea of a "bird room." He had just such a walk-in aviary at his home, where he accommodated up to two hundred bird species. As his biographer, Bernhard Schneider, explained, this allowed him to "carry out the studies essential to writing his books in close proximity to the birds, either from a chair next to the glass front door or sitting comfortably on a carefully covered sofa inside the aviary itself." Reportedly, this over-the-top bird lover even slept either inside or right next to his home aviary.

Russ succeeded in breeding ninety-two species, including sixty-one that had never been bred in Europe before. These included not only strawberry, spice, and zebra finches, but also Bengalese or society finches and red-billed leiothrix (also known as Pekin robins). To procure suitable birds, Russ relied on his connections with the Hagenbecks, a close-knit clan of bird traders. He, in turn, sold some of his own birds via classified advertisements to help recoup his expenses. Finally, he opened his home aviary to interested ornithologists, keeping strict opening hours for his "shrine." When mice became a persistent problem, he trained a special "aviary cat" to keep the little rodents in check. His frequent moves around Berlin probably had something to do with the use to which he intended to put his accommodations:

Time and time again, just as I have rented an apartment, the land-lord backs out of the agreement at the last minute as soon as he hears that I want to devote one room solely to the upkeep of living birds.

THE IDEA OF having a room reserved for birds—either in your home or as a separate structure—was soon copied by bird lovers in Germany, the Netherlands, Switzerland, Hungary, Russia, and North America. One such bird lover was Prince Ferdinand I (1861–1948). In his youth, Ferdinand joined a research expedition to Brazil, and he is credited with being the first person to breed birds such as bush petronias, Sudan golden sparrows, and paradise parrots.

Ferdinand's life was often unsettled. After Bulgaria achieved independence from the Ottoman Empire, he became prince regnant in 1887 and tsar in 1908, before going into exile in Coburg, Germany, after World War I. Later, he undertook more expeditions to East Africa, Egypt, and the Sudan. Throughout all these changes in fortune, large birdhouses full of a variety of breeding birds were a constant in his life, and, in the end, about one hundred aviaries adorned the gardens around his country house. Soon, generously proportioned cages that allowed birds some room to fly—so-called flight cages—became fashionable as a more manageable alternative to bird rooms or aviaries, which required a great deal of space.

Aviculture became more popular with the advent of businesses that specialized in acclimatizing birds to conditions in their new countries of residence. The birds were caught in their countries of origin with no regard for loss of life. They then endured months-long ocean journeys in abominable conditions. They were usually housed in large cages equipped with a few perches with lattice nailed to the front. There was virtually no light or air. Their food consisted of bananas, oranges, and potatoes thrown into the cage. Many did not survive this torture. Germany, meanwhile, became an exporter of canaries bred in that country. Two firms, Carl Reiche and Ludwig Ruhe, both located near Hannover, sold male canaries to the United States, South America, Great Britain, Russia, and Australia.

The most ridiculous arguments were trotted out to justify keeping songbirds—often in solitary confinement. "The birds prefer having a small space all to themselves to sharing a large space. The cage is theirs alone, so they can groom themselves without interference." Some people did object, though, saying it was obvious that caged birds were depressed because their songs changed. Instead of joyful woodland melodies, they sang dirges to mourn their lost freedom. Despite the initial protests, after a few decades, few continued to object to the practice.

FOLLOWING SPREAD
Karl Russ's legendary bird room

{ 6 }

Lost in the Mists of Time

ALONGSIDE THE HIGHLY decorated scientists and adventurers who traveled to the ends of the world are others who have earned their place in the imaginary lineage of bird lovers even though they often toiled away in obscurity. They are the supporting cast to those driven to discover why birds are the way they are, patient observers content to capture birds' likenesses or simply record what they saw. Marcus zum Lamm (1544–1606) was a Protestant cleric at the court of the prince electors of the palatinate in Heidelberg, Germany. As a Renaissance humanist, he was interested in the workings of the natural world. His work, *Thesaurus picturarum* (Thesaurus in Pictures), extended to thirty-three volumes and covered all manner of animals; however, the opulent watercolor illustrations and attendant high printing costs of the three volumes on birds afford them a special place in the collection. They formed an important foundation for knowledge of birds in Central Europe in the sixteenth century.

Lamm probably began studying birds in 1564, when he stopped to observe a great white pelican he spied while on his way to his place of work in Poitiers. He was particularly interested in the link between the weather and changes in the plant and animal world. The twentieth-century zoologist Ragnar Kinzelbach explained Lamm's quest: "The attempt to recognize changes in Nature and therefore God's will in a timely manner using portents such as the appearance of unusual birds is religiously motivated."

Lamm's observations are an early example of what today we call biomonitoring or phenology—that is to say, keeping detailed records of plant and animal life in order to be able to track environmental changes.

Lamm drew from sources that were less than reliable, including hearsay, skins of dead birds, or other people's illustrations. He included not only real birds—mostly from the area around Heidelberg and Speyer—but also fabulous birds, such as the griffin, and real birds to which he attached fabulous stories, such as the dancing, harlequin-colored male ruff. For example, he interpreted the appearance of this "puffed-up, scaly devil-bird," as he described it, as a portent for the arrival of animals from foreign lands. Shortly before his death, he drew a dove, a bird that symbolized the Holy Spirit.

WE KNOW LITTLE about the life of Eleazar Albin (1690–1742), who taught drawing in London. He published *A Natural History of Birds*, the first British book to contain multiple color plates, which, he claimed, were etched using live birds as models. However, the birds come across as so stiff and lifeless that this seems unlikely. Albin was keen on being comprehensive, and he urged his readers to bring any interesting birds they found to his house "next to the Dog and Duck on the Tottenham Court Road."

THE DUTCH PAINTER Roelandt Savery (1576 or 1578–1639) has bequeathed to us the most extraordinary paintings of birds. In one of his bird-filled dreamscapes, about fifty different feathered

"Devil bird" by Marcus zum Lamm

Landscape with Birds by Roelandt Savery

creatures that would certainly never have been found together in nature romp around a fantastical landscape in no identifiable geographic location. He transcended nature, collecting together whatever birds took his fancy, using the landscape as a backdrop against which to display them. He included ostriches and parrots, and there is even a lively dodo in his remarkable assemblage, a bird the Dutch would have first seen in 1598 when they discovered the island of Mauritius. The ground and the air are filled with birds and nothing but birds—there is not a squirrel or deer in sight. His older brother had taught him how to paint birds, fish, and four-footed creatures, but he did not turn his attention to the other members of the animal kingdom until later in his creative life.

ON JOHANN JACOB Hübner's (1761–1826) gravestone, which used to stand in the Protestant cemetery in the Bavarian town of Augsburg, it states that he was a "student of nature." Hübner was one of the last practitioners of copper engraving in Augsburg. He left behind his *Sammlung auserlesener Vögel und Schmetterlinge* (Collection of Choice Birds and Butterflies), dated 1793. On each of the one hundred copper plates, he drew a single bird, every one accompanied by a butterfly or moth. The illustrations are not particularly detailed, and it is clear that he was acquainted with many of the birds only from other artists' renditions. Despite that, his work is charming because he granted himself a certain artistic liberty. In some cases— for instance, in his portrait of a swan—it looks as though the bird and the insect (in this case, a copper butterfly) are not only aware of each other but also actively communicating. In his engraving of a hawk owl, the pattern of the bird's plumage appears only slightly modified on the wings of the accompanying moth. And is that Cuban Amazon hiding in the background on page 68—a bird Hübner called a "white-headed parrot"—really about to throw a cherry at the moth that shares the picture?

An unnamed friend left us this pithy character sketch of Hübner, which conjures up a striking image:

> *He crouched over slightly as he walked. His general appearance had an engagingly provocative charm. His slightly pointed nose, his small beady eyes, his prominent teeth, and his too-wide mouth gave him an almost ironic expression. He kept to himself and lived quietly and removed from society. I still recall his knowledgeable companionship with pleasure.*

{ 7 }

Championing Birds

ACCORDING TO THE much-repeated story, this is what Saint Francis of Assisi (1181 or 1182–1226), born Francesco di Bernardone, once said when he preached to birds:

My brother and sister birds, you should praise your Creator and always love Him: He gave you feathers for clothes, wings to fly and all other things that you need. It is God who made you noble among all creatures, making your home in thin, pure air. Without sowing or reaping, you receive God's guidance and protection.

Then the birds stretched out their necks, spread their wings, opened their beaks, and looked toward the monk. When he walked among them, his habit brushed over their heads and bodies before he blessed them, made the sign of the cross over them, and instructed them to fly away. Saint Francis was a champion of birds par excellence. He pronounced that no one should catch, kill, or otherwise harm larks, and it is said that he built nests for turtle doves with his own hands.

SINCE SAINT FRANCIS, there have been many people who have devoted their lives to championing birds. Instead of collecting eggs or shooting birds as many of his contemporaries were doing, Henry David Thoreau (1817–62) was patiently honing his ability to concentrate on and observe the many and varied connections between animals and plants. One of his ongoing interests was tracking the role birds played in distributing seeds. He was a pioneer of intensely focused bird watching outdoors, undertaking this activity decades before birders began consulting the first pocket guidebooks, roaming woods and fields with cameras at the ready, or holding out tape recorders, their hearts set on capturing avian melodies. As binoculars had not yet been invented, he was content with a simple "spyglass"—a kind of telescope used in the military and for navigation at the time. Thoreau knew Wilson's and Audubon's books, of course, and those of a few other writers, and he used them to help him identify the birds he saw. His records were not ordered in any particular way. He just jotted down what he saw, so, inevitably, his notes about when birds arrived and when they made their nests were often repetitious. As the years went by, he gradually compiled a list of all the local birds he had observed. For some species, such as the buntings, he struggled to identify exactly which ones they were, but this in no way suggests any deficiencies in his powers of observation, because later observers with access to vastly superior equipment than he had still had great difficulty telling them apart.

Thoreau's lists are valuable, but it is the unusual thoughts and associations bird watching sparked in him that are so fascinating to read, even today.

I once had a sparrow alight on my shoulder for a moment while I was hoeing in a village garden, and I felt that I was more distinguished by that circumstance than I should have been by any epaulet I could have worn.

Saint Francis of Assisi

He would probably have agreed with contemporary birder Vernon Head, who wrote, "To see a bird, we must enter its habitat completely; we must connect emotionally," and he frequently emphasized the particular connection he felt with the natural phenomena he observed. The long, drawn-out cry of the loon reminded

Henry David Thoreau

him of a person calling out and, in an unexpected twist, of a sound he himself made: "I have heard a sound exactly like it when breathing heavily through my own nostrils, half awake at ten at night, suggesting my affinity to the loon; as if its language were but a dialect of my own."

Thoreau saw his native Concord, Massachusetts, as a microcosm of the world, and he felt immense pride whenever he read about a plant or animal that lived in a far-off country that he then spied in his own surroundings. "It is not worth the while to go round the world to count the *cats* in *Zanzibar*," he once wrote with evident satisfaction. At the time, he had the great good fortune to be able to observe birds in natural surroundings that were still largely intact, although he was already worried about possible threats. To this day, the area around Concord, Thoreau's hometown, is one of the most thoroughly researched patches of land in all of North America.

TOWARD THE END of the nineteenth century, decades after Thoreau had made his observations, wildlife conservationists began to target bird hunting in all its various forms. The bird conservation movement arose around the same time in many different countries. That was when people who championed birds realized that they had to band together to find a wider audience for their message so that they could call for conservation measures from governments and better inform the public of the birds' plight. As a result of their efforts, the general public began to change the way it looked at birds, which now became symbols of nature and beauty. It was hoped that working for their preservation would help ward off the ravages of unchecked industrialization. Here are just a few of the people who played prominent roles in this movement.

Baron Hans Hermann von Berlepsch (1857–1933) is considered to be the father of German bird conservation. In his pamphlet *Der gesamte Vogelschutz* (Complete Bird Conservation), he railed against sentimental behavior when dealing with birds. He was much more concerned with the practical benefits of protecting birds, which he declared to be "the appointed guardians of the balance between the plant and insect worlds." He understood bird conservation to be, above all, an important economic endeavor, and referred to the *Convention for the Protection of Birds Useful to Agriculture* signed by twelve European states in Paris in 1902. Italy was not a signatory, but, in the light of recent "insect calamities," Berlepsch was hopeful that the country might yet join. He had seen for himself the mass destruction of migrating birds in that country and decried the toll on native bird populations. Cats that roamed freely there also posed a danger to birds.

Berlepsch introduced a distinction between "useful" birds (which included nocturnal birds of prey and birds that climbed) and "harmful" birds (starlings and diurnal birds of prey). He also complained about the loss of natural nesting habitats and stressed that the highest priority must be given to woodlands especially suitable for the protection of birds. These woods were a mixture of hawthorn, hornbeam, wild rose, common gooseberry, wild currants, and, where appropriate, Tatarian honeysuckle. Berlepsch also wanted to provide nesting boxes modeled on the cavities made by great spotted woodpeckers for all cavity-nesting birds to use. One of the boxes' special features was their entrances, which always faced southeast. The entrance holes—all of a specific size—were slightly angled to keep rain from entering the boxes. The walls were thick to provide insulation and uneven on the inside to give the birds something to cling to. The breeding cavity was bottle-shaped and ended in a pointed trough. Following the translation of his pamphlet, "Von Berlepsch bird boxes" became famous the world over. And when Berlepsch had his moated castle renovated, he had "nesting stones" built into the walls. In 1908, he created a bird sanctuary that was recognized as the first of its kind. Fittingly enough, on his grave in a churchyard in Seebach, Thuringia, stands a birdbath.

EARLY IN THE 1940s, people realized that whooping crane numbers were plummeting and the birds were threatened with extinction. There was talk at the time of just fifteen birds remaining. The Cooperative Whooping Crane Project came into being in 1945, and soon after, Robert Porter Allen (1905–63), an ornithologist associated with the National Audubon Society, was put in charge. For many years, Allen devoted himself to rescuing these impressive birds. He followed them on their migration route from the American South to the Arctic Circle to find their secret nesting grounds.

An American author named Kathleen Kaska documented Allen's story in her book *The Man Who Saved the Whooping Crane.*

THE CANADIAN ORNITHOLOGIST George Archibald, who cofounded the International Crane Foundation and was once its president, developed a unique relationship with a whooping crane called Tex. This female was born in the zoo in San Antonio, Texas, in 1967. She had health problems, which meant that she had to be raised by hand, isolated from others of her kind. During this period of intensive care, she became imprinted on humans, and all attempts to persuade her to mate failed. She was simply not interested in laying eggs. In 1975, Archibald came up with the idea of building on his close relationship with the bird by taking on, as best he could, the role of a male. He spent many months at the bird's side and repeatedly performed mating dances in the hopes of encouraging her to lay. Meanwhile, Tex was artificially inseminated several times. The following spring, Tex, who was by then about ten years old, laid an egg. Unfortunately, the egg was infertile. The egg she laid the next spring was fertile, but the embryo died before it hatched. Finally, when she laid a third egg in May 1981, it was removed from the nest and a dummy egg was put in its place. The crane chick that hatched a month later, a little boy, was given the name Gee Whiz. This crane—who has since grown to be an old man—fathered offspring that now live free and participate in the birds' annual migrations. Archibald has taken to jokingly calling these youngsters his grandchildren. And sometimes he even travels in pursuit of cranes—checking on other members of the extended family, as it were—including a visit to Bhutan in South Asia, a major wintering habitat for some of the whoopers' black-necked relatives.

IT IS QUITE something to retreat to a South Pacific island 500 miles (800 kilometers) off the coast of Chile for weeks without an

Internet connection to surround yourself with millions of sea birds. Since his influential essay "My Bird Problem," the American writer Jonathan Franzen has become arguably the most famous bird watcher of our time. He almost never misses an opportunity to point out how close to his heart these creatures fly. Whenever he travels, he always researches the best birding places beforehand. In a long talk to students about the unpleasant side effects of mobile phones and smartphones, Franzen revealed that at some point in his life, he fell in love with birds.

> *I did this not without significant resistance, because it is very uncool to be a birdwatcher, because anything that betrays real passion is by definition uncool. But little by little, in spite of myself, I developed this passion, and although one half of a passion is obsession, the other half is love. And so, yes, I kept a meticulous list of the birds I'd seen, and, yes, I went to inordinate lengths to see new species. But, no less important, whenever I looked at a bird, any bird, even a pigeon or a sparrow, I could feel my heart overflow with love.*

Franzen has passionately dedicated himself to the fight against the songbird hunt in the Mediterranean. Every imaginable small bird is hunted there using shotguns, nets, and—as if that were not enough—a natural adhesive called *cordia myxa* or "glue berry," which is smeared on posts. In the course of this hunt, not only targeted birds, such as song thrushes and blackcaps, are caught, but also turtle doves, nightingales, and even chameleons. On the island of Cyprus alone, where the hunt can be traced as far back as the sixteenth century, more than one hundred species and an estimated two million individual birds are caught every year. Along the Egyptian coast, from the border with Libya to the Sinai Peninsula, bird hunters hang nets to catch birds. These nets, which are 10 to 12 feet (several meters) high and extend for almost 450 miles (700

Cerulean warbler

kilometers), are designed to snare birds exhausted by their flight over the Mediterranean Sea. Only those birds that have the strength to fly higher—cuckoos, for example—escape the treacherous barrier. It is estimated that more than 140 million birds are caught in these nets every year and then sold in markets as delicacies. Many of those birds are on the International Union for Conservation of Nature's Red List and are threatened with extinction. All these efforts to catch birds have broken Franzen's heart. He says, "The blue of the Mediterranean isn't pretty to me anymore." His groundbreaking essay "Emptying the Skies," originally published in the *New Yorker*, has been made into a documentary movie.

In Franzen's novel *Freedom*, the fate of a cerulean warbler plays an important role in the story of an American family. This small blue bird's numbers have diminished by more than 80 percent since 1966 thanks to deforestation of both South American rainforests—winter quarters for the bird, which otherwise spends its time in North America—and the woods where it breeds. Franzen comes out swinging and points to American consumer habits and the hunger for coal as an energy source. The book culminates in a story that is, in part, a parable about the problems facing people who try to make the "right" decisions given the realities of contemporary life.

Bird lover Walter Berglund—one of the main characters in Franzen's novel—gets embroiled in an argument with his cat-owning neighbors. (House cats in the United States alone kill an estimated one million songbirds every day. Birds' natural defense mechanisms are not well developed where house cats are concerned, because they were only introduced a few hundred years ago and neither wild cats, such as pumas, nor other natural predators have ever posed a comparable danger to birds.) So Berglund tries to persuade the people in his neighborhood to keep a closer eye on their cats and stop them prowling around. When that doesn't work, he catches his neighbor's tomcat and takes it to an animal shelter. But other cats are quickly acquired. Berglund is fighting an impossible fight. Finally, he declares his weekend retreat a bird sanctuary and surrounds it with a high fence to keep the cats out.

Are there people who love both cats and birds, or is that an insoluble contradiction? This opens up a difficult, emotionally charged field. Why is it that corvids such as magpies and carrion crows are viewed negatively as nest robbers, but domestic cats that catch birds do not have this reputation? It is quite a paradox that people who feed stray cats believe they are doing a particularly good deed to help protect animals, even though it is well known that these strays have an inordinately large number of birds on their conscience.

FRANZEN SHARES HIS concern about birds as especially sensitive inhabitants of this planet with Australian Peter Doherty, who won a Nobel Prize for medicine. Doherty believes that the welfare of birds is inextricably entwined with the fate of human beings and regards birds as an early-warning system for threats to the ecological health and well-being of Earth—assuming people pick up on and heed the warning signals.

You do not have to look far back in the past for examples. In spring 2014, golden-winged warblers had no sooner arrived in their North American breeding grounds in Appalachia than they moved right out again. Thanks to their "flight"—over the course of the next five days they put over 900 miles (1,500 kilometers) behind them—they escaped a powerful approaching tornado that likely would have killed them. We know birds sense very slight changes in atmospheric pressure, yet at the time the birds left, there was absolutely no obvious meteorological indication of the impending disaster. Henry Streby, an environmental scientist who was tracking the birds' flight paths using miniature geolocators attached to their backs, just happened to observe the birds' behavior. Storms produce very low-frequency sounds that can reverberate for thousands of miles, and Streby attributes the warblers' prudent action to their ability to sense infrasonic sound waves generated by the approaching tornado.

Observations such as these support the suggestion that birds are capable of picking up on dangers that will also affect us sooner or later if we do not take measures to protect ourselves. Birds play an important role as environmental indicators, and some of the impacts of climate change can be assessed by observing changes in their distribution, abundance, and migratory behavior.

BIRD WATCHING AND wanting to protect birds are, of course, not mutually exclusive activities. What made Ernest Harold Baynes (1868–1925) so remarkable was that he did both with such superlative good humor that he attracted large numbers of people to his cause, making him one of the most important, if not the most important, American bird conservationist of his day.

Baynes was born in Calcutta and grew up in England. He immigrated to the United States with his parents, worked for a short time for the *New York Times,* and all his life was a great advocate for all manner of animals. His house was surrounded by foxes, raccoons, wolves, bears, and bison. He maintained a relationship with all of them, although he was closer to some than to others. He had no formal scientific training, but that did not stop him from transforming himself into a "wildlife showman" with a gift for connecting with audiences around his passion. In 1910, after giving a lecture on birds in Meriden, Connecticut, he encouraged the townspeople to create a bird club. The following year, thanks to a generous donation from the author Helen Woodruff Smith, the club bought an abandoned farm and created one of the first bird sanctuaries in the United States. Meriden soon got the name "Bird Village," and the Helen Woodruff Smith Bird Sanctuary exists to this day.

The club imported 150 Von Berlepsch bird boxes from Germany. Massive stones, all with depressions at the top to collect water for the birds to drink, were brought in from the surrounding countryside. A friend of Baynes, Percy MacKaye, wrote a short theatrical piece, "Sanctuary: A Bird Masque," to be played at the opening for the sanctuary in 1913. Margaret Wilson, the daughter of the president of the Meriden Bird Club, played the part of a bird spirit and sang "The Hermit Thrush" from behind some shrubbery, while her sister, Nell, wearing a bird mask, played the part of the bird being pursued by a hunter. Baynes then took the piece on a cross-country tour to promote bird conservation. (In those days, feathers were still popular adornments for ladies' hats.) Baynes helped found numerous bird clubs as he felt they were the most effective way to ensure the conservation of birds. These clubs not only helped the birds, they also helped create a sense of community among their members, who might otherwise never have met up with like-minded people.

Baynes based his book *Wild Bird Guests*, which appeared in 1915, on his experiences in Meriden. He recalled the harsh winter when many of the hundreds of pine grosbeaks that flew in from the north came and sat on his hand or on his shoulder to be fed. And he reminisced about the crossbills that arrived another winter and hung around for so long that they came to be a daily source of entertainment.

> *We went out to play with them for a while almost every day, and by and by they seemed to look for our coming. We would sit on the well-trampled snow we had prepared for their feeding ground, and from the trees about us they would come down in a musical shower, to alight upon our heads and shoulders and to feed from our hands. It was such fun that sometimes even when the thermometer registered from ten to fifteen degrees below zero we would sit there feeding them,*

photographing them, or often simply watching them, until we were
almost too numb to get up.

Baynes wrote about the dangers songbirds faced and how best
to counteract them. His goal was to recruit a whole army of "bird
defenders," and he wanted to do so from the ranks of people who up
until this time had been "bird destroyers." The key to his message
was to get people to see the birds in their gardens as their guests. If
they were guests, then the sacrosanct rule of hospitality would apply.

It is not possible for us to be indifferent to the welfare of our invited
guests. The moment a person—be it a man or a bird—has accepted
our hospitality, has broken bread with us, has eaten our salt, our
relations towards that person have changed.

To this day, people who set out food for birds in their gardens—
or, better yet, who grow the kinds of plants and attract the kinds of
insects that birds love to feed on—feel intimately connected with
their visitors and want nothing more than to see them enjoying
themselves.

{ 8 }

In the Company of Birds

HERE WERE, AND still are, people who seek the company of birds for years, decades, or even most of their lives without thinking there is anything odd about their behavior. Robert Stroud (1890–1963) pursued his hobby in a highly unusual environment: a prison cell. After he killed a rival in a dispute over his girlfriend, whom he supposedly pimped as a prostitute, he spent more than half a century in various penitentiaries in the United States. While he was in a federal maximum security prison in Leavenworth, Kansas, he started breeding canaries—about three hundred of them. He studied their behavior and physiology, developed a handful of cures for bird diseases, and wrote a couple of books that earned him the respect of the ornithological community. He is said to have become interested in birds after finding an injured sparrow in the prison courtyard. Unfortunately, he allowed his canaries to range freely in his prison cell, which led to serious hygiene problems. When prison authorities ordered an end to his activities, an acquaintance (who later became his wife) campaigned on his behalf and collected fifty thousand signatures on a petition that turned the tide in his favor: not only was Stroud allowed to continue breeding canaries, he even got a second cell for his program. The discovery that he was using some of his equipment to brew alcohol was the final straw for the authorities in Kansas, and he was transferred to Alcatraz. Oddly enough, he went down in history as the "Birdman of Alcatraz," even though he was no longer given the resources to breed birds after his transfer. In fact, he was expressly forbidden to pursue his avocation.

A PARTICULARLY WELL-DOCUMENTED example of a person living in the company of birds (thanks to his biography, *The Living Air*) is the story of Jean Delacour (1890–1985). Next to his bed in his wealthy parents' Paris apartment was a box that held a fluffy white chick, which quickly became his most prized possession as he recovered from a long illness at the age of three. Delacour himself credited the chick with hastening the healing process. He observed every movement and reaction of the tiny bird, which soon grew into a handsome hen with a beard and black neck and tail. It was henceforth referred to as *le poulet de Monsieur Jean* ("Master Jean's hen"). The hen belonged to a little-known breed called *faverolle herminé*, and Delacour was able to follow its fortunes for a good number of years at his family's farmyard in Villers-Bretonneux, where it had been sent to live in the company of hundreds of other hens. It remained remarkably tame and reportedly always recognized him.

That was not the end of the story, however, for the young Delacour soon developed an interest in exotic birds: Asiatic pheasants, various guinea fowl found in different parts of Africa, and miniature chickens called bantams.

I could not imagine that anything more wonderful could possibly exist. Sitting in the shade of the old cherry tree, so friendly and protective, I spent hours watching my birds. It was a never-ending

source of delight; I knew every individual, its history, its peculiari-
ties, its temper and its personal record. My head was burdened with
bird problems; their tragedies, comedies, dramas of love and jealousy,
which I tried to interpret, filled my thoughts.

Over the years, Delacour constructed several birdhouses on
the family estate, built an enclosure especially for ostriches, and
had a large pond installed in front of his house, where ducks and
swans soon moved in. Now he could observe the activity of wild
birds directly from his window, and he was entertained by birdsong until late into the night. A large, heated birdhouse comprising
forty-seven aviaries followed. It was a miniature paradise.

The cages could not be seen from the outside; you opened a door near
the end of a long wall, screened by trees and shrubs, and suddenly
you found yourself surrounded by birds. You walked along straight
paths, all lined with flowers; each compartment was a little garden in
which gorgeous birds showed to full advantage. The cages were varied
in shape and size; here and there, other paths began, affording new
vistas. At a turn one entered the indoor gallery, with its rows of cages,
and it looked like a library of birds, showing among tropical plants.
Even in these early years one could see there hummingbirds, sunbirds,
and birds of paradise, then very unusual.

Near and far around Villers-Bretonneux, Delacour was surrounded by other people who were passionate about birds and who
intensified his interest in them. His network branched out in so
many directions, it is impossible to mention them all. The banker
and butterfly collector Eugène Boullet (1847–1923) was one of his
acquaintances. Despite having a physical handicap that limited his
mobility, he made many trips to India, the Middle East, and North
Africa, returning with birds, plants, and other exotic souvenirs. He

kept honeyeaters, sugarbirds, leafbirds (also known as fruitsuckers), parrots, doves, and mynahs (a talkative bird in the starling family native to the Indian subcontinent) in his spacious home. The birds were all so tame that he often let them fly around inside. He had flamingoes in his garden and a pond filled with black-necked swans, geese, ducks, cranes, screamers, and scarlet ibis. Through Boullet, Delacour got to know Charles Debreuil, who maintained a number of gardens connected by a complex system of tunnels in Melun, south of Paris. Apart from many rare plants, trees, fish, and mammals, he also had an outstanding collection of pheasants, pigeons, parrots, cranes, and waterfowl. Debreuil's particular interest was the South American rhea, which at first glance resembles an ostrich. Delacour also mentioned one Madame E. Lécallier, who had collected thousands of parrots, pigeons, pheasants, and waterfowl at her estate in Normandy. Everyone he knew had their own particular bird obsession.

Toward the end of World War I, the garden at Villers was destroyed, but Delacour soon purchased the Château de Clères in Normandy and quickly set about adapting the garden and grounds for his birds and other animals. Later, he proudly claimed that up until 1940, there was probably no other place in the world where so many rare species were gathered together as there were in the gardens at Clères. There were three thousand birds, belonging to more than five hundred species, most of which he had collected during expeditions to India, Indochina, China, Japan, Madagascar, and the Caribbean. He carefully chose birds that would not damage plants in the garden and specifically avoided birds of prey and fish-eating waterfowl. Despite these restrictions, he had more than one hundred species of waterfowl alone. Clères became an attraction for nature lovers from all four corners of the world until, in 1940, thirty-two bombs from the German air force inflicted severe damage on life in the park. Delacour immigrated to the United

7. *Oroshuhn. (Crypturus.)*   9. *Perlhuhn. (Meleagris.)*   8. *Baumhuhn. (Crax.)*

10. *Hahn. (Gallus.)*

11. *Truthahn. (Gallo pavo.)*

12. *Pfau. (Pavo.)*

States, became an American citizen, worked in the Los Angeles County Museum, and, like the old-school citizen of the world that he was, commuted back and forth between the United States and Europe for many years. In 1947, the park at Clères was reopened to the public. It exists to this day.

ALFRED EZRA (1872–1955), another friend of Delacour, was considered to be a specialist in the breeding of exotic birds. Thanks to a concoction of honey, milk, and Mellin's Food for Infants and Invalids—a close substitute for human breast milk—he successfully kept nectar-feeding birds in captivity. Delacour accompanied Ezra on journeys not only to his country of birth—India—but also to Egypt and the Middle East. At Foxwarren Park in Surrey, southwest of London, Ezra kept Indian antelope, wallabies, and a number of different species of deer. All kinds of waterfowl, cranes, and game birds mingled peacefully in the enclosures. In a clearing in a stand of larches, he set up numerous smaller enclosures complete with heated shelters where he kept small birds, pigeons, and parrots. He also managed a bird clinic. One of Ezra's specialties was breeding Indian rose-ringed parakeets. The birds had been known in Europe for centuries, and Ezra's breeding program succeeded in producing a lutino, or "yellow albino," much prized by wealthy Indian princes, who were ready to pay large amounts for these lovely light-yellow birds.

Ezra was known as an extremely good-natured and generous animal lover. His most unusual habit was keeping birds in his bedroom—hummingbirds, sunbirds, white-rumped shamas, Persian nightingales, and other small songbirds—and he always had little cages set out for them on his bedroom tables and windowsills. Although he was a busy man with many responsibilities, he prided himself on looking after his birds himself. He let them fly free in enclosed spaces so they could get their exercise, and he taught them—no one knew how—to return to their cages when they were done. Sadly, World War II inflicted severe damage on his collection, although he kept a series of birds up until his death.

PETER MARKHAM SCOTT (1909–89) moved in Delacour's outer circle. An artist, seafarer, and glider pilot, he began to study the behavior of geese and ducks near an abandoned English lighthouse on the Norfolk coast. After World War II, he launched the Wildfowl Trust. Its goal—which it achieved—was to research waterfowl in as much detail as possible. Many species of birds threatened with extinction were successfully bred in captivity, and thanks to this organization, Scott became well regarded as a conservationist.

OSKAR HEINROTH (1871–1945) and his first wife, Magdalena (1883–1932), met at the zoological museum in Berlin. For years, they worked on a monumental book that they started in 1908 with photographs of a breeding pair of nightjars in their apartment. They conceived a plan to become acquainted with the birds of Germany from the time the chicks hatched through to adulthood. Their plan was to measure and describe physical changes as the birds matured and, through observation, get some idea of what might be going on inside their heads.

Almost continuous observation was the basis for their experiments into and investigation of bird psychology. They felt they were well placed to distinguish between innate behaviors and those behaviors "individuals must learn through experience." Working with hundreds of birds, however, came at a price: for example, vacations were hardly ever possible as raising birds in a "nursery" required round-the-clock supervision. By some accounts, though, their intense work schedule saved them from becoming complete "fools for birds." Amateur devotees usually owned only a few caged birds and therefore enjoyed a much lighter workload than the harried

Magdalena Heinroth
with an owl

Heinroths, who claimed they were not given to either anthropomor-
phizing or sentimentality. In their opinion, people who found young
or small birds cute or delightful had no appreciation of science, and
well-meaning, tender-hearted visitors drove them to distraction.

However, their business-like approach did not prevent the Heinroths from deriving great joy from the company of their birds or
from devoting themselves to solving the numerous puzzles they
presented. Working with what they had, they advanced the somewhat questionable idea that animals kept in captivity can be used
as a benchmark for the behavior of their wild relatives. The result
of their collaboration was *The Birds,* a four-volume work with three
thousand photographs of individual birds they had known.

ANOTHER RESEARCHER INTO bird psychology was Konrad
Lorenz (1903–89). There's no way of knowing whether Lorenz
would ever have become a pioneer of behavioral research if he
hadn't read *The Wonderful Adventures of Nils Holgersson,* a story
about a little boy who hitched a ride on the back of a farm goose
to accompany wild geese on their migration. Even Lorenz couldn't

remember whether his encounter with real live wild geese preceded his reading of Selma Lagerlöf's book or whether it was the other way around. When he was an old man, he wrote, "Both experiences happened in my young life at about the same time. The order in which they happened doesn't really matter." Whatever the case may be, the behavioral scientist thought Lagerlöf went too far in describing the birds as though they were people.

As a young boy, Lorenz watched ducklings as they cheerfully waddled about. He gave two of them names—Pipsa and Pupsa—and so began his lifelong interest in ducks, geese, and swans. He wrote what he jokingly called his first "scientific" paper about a tame jackdaw called Tschok that was part of a breeding colony he had observed for decades. Every so often, he took in sick animals from the Vienna Zoo and nursed them back to health. After pursuing studies in medicine and zoology, Lorenz proved that although young birds are born with instinctive behaviors, for a limited time early in their life they learn particular patterns of behavior that are extremely difficult to erase later. He also discovered that there are considerable differences between species. For example, he observed that newly hatched curlews wanted nothing to do with him as a surrogate father, because the chicks are born knowing how to recognize their parents and human beings are not on their radar. It turned out to be quite another thing with greylag geese.

When Lorenz discovered that greylag chicks imprinted on him in the absence of their parents, he came closer to the birds than anyone ever thought possible. His relationship with the goslings earned him the title "Father Goose." And he appeared to take his parental role seriously, not considering it beneath him to swim in a pond with a flock of goslings; indeed, he seemed to enjoy the experience immensely. Lorenz either did not know or did not want to know that imprinting, like other forms of learned behavior, can be reversed. He received a Nobel Prize for his research in 1973. We do not know

if the geese that imprinted on him were abandoned to their fate
after they had fulfilled their scientific purpose. Did he simply use
them to develop his behavioral theories? But given the millions of
fattened geese that are led to slaughter every year, perhaps it doesn't
really matter.

THE CULTURAL CRITIC and author Friedrich Georg Jünger (1898–
1977) nurtured an almost religious relationship with birds, as did
his brother, Ernst, although to a somewhat lesser extent. (Ernst
went on to be a philosopher and preferred beetles.) Birds were for
them the one constant in a dramatically changing world. At his parents' house, Jünger dedicated a whole room to birds. This is how his
biographer, Jörg Magenau, described the importance of birds in the
young boy's life:

> *They were his friends. His joy. Friedrich even wanted to trace the
> trails of birds in the sky. He talked to birds, and he knew all the birds
> that lived in the water, the sky and the woods of Lake Constance out-
> side his window... He took on the rhythm of the birds, he lived with
> them, and he carried them with him into his dreams. He decorated the
> walls of his room with pictures of birds. A built-in cupboard held the
> jewels of his collection. He stored them in metal cash boxes and was
> proud to display their contents: feathers and eggs, rocks and gnarled
> roots. Brehm's book on birds stood at the ready... Fritz [Friedrich]
> eavesdropped on birds and watched them fly so he could track down
> their hiding places. He knew about the barn owl's roost under the
> chimney and the nuthatch's nesting hole in the old oak with a densely
> leaved canopy that towered above all the other trees and the house.*

And that was not all. Jünger also noted the dates when migratory birds arrived and when they left—storks, grey geese, swallows,
swifts, lapwings, and cranes. When thousands of cranes flew by in

their V formations on their way to southern Europe or Africa, he lay on his back in the grass listening to their plaintive calls and crying because he was so moved by this wonder of Nature.

He understood that collecting birds flew in the face of truly understanding them.

You must try to observe birds from a distance and approach them carefully without frightening them. You have to keep them alive in your memory. To be beautiful, they must live, stretch their wings, and lift their voices. When they die, their feathers lose their luster.

Later in his life, he rejected the idea of evolution as he was reluctant to apply the concept of development and progress to Nature, preferring, perhaps, to think of it as already perfect.

Birds seemed to form a personalized backdrop as world events left their mark on Jünger's life. After enlisting in the army during World War I, he was shot in the shoulder and lung. As he convalesced, flocks of swifts surrounded his room. Every spring, when he heard the first call of that herald of rebirth, the cuckoo, he stole away into the woods. A room in his house in Überlingen on Lake Constance, where he had settled in 1942 and where he entertained such guests as the philosopher Martin Heidegger, soon included a "gallery of feathers." The feathers—a colorful parrot feather, a flight feather from a golden pheasant, a wing feather from a guinea fowl, and a striped blue-black feather from a jay—were framed behind glass and displayed like miniature pieces of art. He ignored the wartime scream of air raid sirens and the rattling of windows as he silently watched peregrines spiraling upward and reflected upon the meaning of birds of prey in the natural world. In contrast to his brother, Ernst, he felt no need, later in life, to take part in drug-fueled fantasy journeys. Just flying up into the air in his mind with the birds was enough for him.

GIVEN THE DIVERSITY of bird life in the world, there is a certain appeal to the idea of intentionally paring down the birds you want to watch to those in your immediate surroundings. Those who do not have a park to call their own often make do with their gardens. Bird watchers who stick close to home can separate regular residents from those who are just dropping by for a visit and study the patterns of their comings and goings. For the British naturalist Gwendolen "Len" Howard (1894–1973), just such a garden was the foundation for her research into the secret lives of birds. She developed what most professional ornithologists would consider to be overly romantic ideas, which she supported with theoretical musings about the peaceful coexistence between people and birds.

After she began a career in London as a musician—she not only played the violin in an orchestra, she also organized concerts for gifted children and gave lessons—she inherited a small piece of land in East Sussex in southeast England in 1942, where she had a house built that she named Dove Cottage. There she lived with the local birds, which often flew inside and nested in her home. She believed that birds are driven not only by instinct but also by intelligence, which is developed to a different degree in each individual. She took many precautions to make sure birds felt safe in her home, and she only let guests in if they were prepared to abide by her strict rules. The garden, too, was mostly arranged to suit the birds' needs. Close by the house, she planted teasels especially for her goldfinches, which loved to perch on them and pick out the seeds.

Naturally, this unconventional lifestyle had its complications.

There are, of course, great difficulties in living as I do, in [the] continual company of numbers of birds. The practical ones are many, such as cleaning up, having things spoilt, the rooms always looking as if prepared for the [chimney] sweep with newspapers spread over furniture and books covered with cloths: then the disturbance of sleep, for they hammer furiously on the panes if I shut the windows at dawn to keep them outside when the nights are short, and they do all they can to prevent my concentrating upon anything except themselves.

The birds kept her busy from dawn to dusk, as she laid out in some detail in her book, *Birds as Individuals.*

They do all they can to hinder any concentrated work,—while I am trying to write this page some are perching on the typewriter, some pulling at my hair, others flying to my hands and falling off as I start to tap the keys.

It was difficult for her to keep on top of the dangers posed to her small charges by her neighbors' cats and marauding jackdaws and magpies. Warding off predators proved to be quite a challenge, and she was not always successful. But, clearly, the pleasure she drew from her life with birds more than compensated for the complications they caused her. Howard went so far as to claim that the birds came to her because they loved her. When a great tit called Twist touched her nose with its beak, she called the gesture a "kiss." She made some astonishing observations about her birds. For example, she believed that a male blackbird had composed a phrase similar to the theme of a rondo in Beethoven's violin concerto. She spent a lot of time recording all their movements, even in their nests, down to the smallest detail. She believed careful observation of individual birds was the key to really understanding them, and she claimed she could tell local great tits apart by their facial expressions, their mannerisms, and their body language.

> *One female Great Tit was under my close observation for six years. She was reared in my neighbour's orchard and mated a bird of the same age from my garden. They reared two broods each year for three years and were a devoted pair, always together, even in winter.*

Howard even drew up a small family tree for her great tits. As well as their dates of birth and death, she meticulously recorded their offspring and "adoptive" children. And she even had her own theory about the birds' vocalizations.

> *I should like to stress the point that birds have a language for their needs, they have recreations, even taking the form of definite games something like ours, they have developed song and use it as a means of expression. In some cases their music is akin to ours.*

She also believed that some birds in her garden were capable of recognizing certain individuals of their own species by their song. She was mostly unimpressed by the opinions of biologists. She lived in a different world—and she had her birds.

OF COURSE, WE can only speculate, but Howard would probably have gotten along very well with the American bird lover Michele Raffin, who is completely at home in a similarly noisy, bird-filled environment. A former Silicon Valley venture capital consultant, she cares for thirty-four different aviaries at her home, where she houses and breeds more than three hundred birds belonging to more than forty exotic and critically endangered species. The controlled chaos of the birds of Pandemonium (as she calls her bird rescue and breeding center) is located in Los Altos, an hour's drive south of San Francisco. Like Howard, Raffin names her birds and is interested in them as individuals with personalities that are both endearing and challenging.

It all started for Raffin when she noticed an injured white dove by the side of a California highway in 1996. At first, she focused on rehabilitating injured birds, but she soon realized that they needed much more help than that. She explains that one of the factors that motivated her to set up her breeding program was the Wild Bird Conservation Act of 1992, which drastically limited the number of wild-caught birds imported into the United States, leading to fewer breeding birds for endangered species in captivity. To address the problem, she increased the number of aviaries at her home and moved into breeding, which, it turns out, she is very good at. The ark that is Pandemonium is keeping hope alive for many exotic birds today.

She ends her book, *The Birds of Pandemonium*, with a description of disadvantaged city children touring her aviaries. That day, the birds, some of which had been known to make her tear her hair out with their antics—Tico, a handsome blue and gold macaw, could be a particular pain—put on a great show:

Any outsider would think these feathered vaudevillians had rehearsed their routine for days. Prank followed prank and wisecrack until the children were breathless with laughter. As the group moved off to have a look at the plum-heads, I stopped for a wary look at Tico. The next group of children would be along in a few minutes, but having just lost his audience, he might pitch a hissy fit. His bloodcurdling screams could scare the arriving children.

But there he sat, calm and silent—a real stand-up guy. We looked at each other through the mesh, and I felt that old connection—fleetingly, but it was enough. He might well try to bite me that evening, but, for the moment, my shoulders relaxed.

As the next group of children approached, Shana put the cherry on top of my morning.

"Hey, pretty mama. I love you!"

And from Tico: "Aw, shut up!"

THE AMERICAN WRITER Paul Bowles (1910–99) lived for a long time in self-imposed exile in Morocco. In his essay "All Parrots Speak," which appeared in the magazine *Holiday* in 1956, he had this to say about people's reactions to his favorite species of bird, the parrot:

A parrot that cannot talk or sing is, we feel, an incomplete parrot. For some reason it fascinates us to see a small, feather-covered creature with a ludicrous, senile face speaking a human language—so much, indeed, that the more simple-minded of us tend to take seriously the idea suggested by our subconscious: that a parrot really is a person (in disguise, of course), but capable of human thought and feeling.

In Mexico and countries in Central America, Bowles watched with fascination as indigenous kitchen staff engaged in monologues that became "dialogues" the moment a parrot threw in a few remarks. For example, as they spent hours fixing their hair, they might ask the bird, "'Do you like it this way?'... and then, changing the position of the tresses, comb in mouth, 'Or like this?'"

Bowles not only taught the birds he owned how to speak, he also believed they knew the meaning of the words they uttered. And so, for him, the birds began to take on the role of human beings.

Parrots in Latin America are rarely kept in cages. Bowles observed that they are monogamous by nature and wrote that they often developed an almost obsessive attachment to a handful of people, all the while subjecting everyone else to either indifference or outright hate. Bowles and his wife developed their first close relationship with a representative of the parrot family when they found themselves stranded in a hotel in Costa Rica, and they ended up purchasing the bird from the owner of the hotel. They named him Budupple, and Bowles seemed to take it all in good humor when the parrot managed not only to destroy (as these birds are wont to do) but also, as unbelievable as it sounds, to eat (without, it seems, experiencing any ill effects) a lens from a pair of opera glasses, a tube of toothpaste, and most of a Russian novel. The only material available to fashion a cage for him was tin. Unfortunately, the parrot whiled away a sea voyage by working on the cage and eventually sawed his way out as Bowles and his wife waited in line at a customs house in Puerto Barrios, Guatemala. The unusually affectionate bird then had the bad manners to poke his head up the skirt of a French woman in the lineup and dig his claws into her fleshy calf as he attempted to climb it, much to the amusement of the other travelers.

Amazingly, these experiences did nothing to dampen Bowles's fascination with these birds. Two years later, in Acapulco, he tried again with a Mexican *cotorro* (a small green parrot). When he discovered

Casuarius, Javanisch Eme, Wird auß Banda ge=
fangen.

Ein Casuarius ist ohngefehr so groß als eine Ziegen,
auf dem Kopf hat er einen Schild von Horn, und
am Halße ist er gestalt wie ein Calcutischer Hahn
mit einem geschlingseten roth und blaw; Er hat kei=
ne Zungen, auch keiner Flügel noch Schwantz, sondern
an statt der Flügel hat er spitzige Stachel, gleich den,
wie von dem Eisen Draten, sie sind aber gantz schlecht,

Ein West=Indianischer Rabe,
Brasilianisch Tracura.

that the bird communicated using a sound that reminded Bowles of the loud honking of an old-fashioned Paris taxi, he decided it would be better to set the bird free. A parakeet called Hitler distinguished itself because it could say *"periquito burro"* ("stupid parakeet"), a name the staff had given him because he tended to strut around in a rage and peck at their bare toes. Although Bowles was fond of the parakeet, he described its personality as "monochromatic." Bowles thought there was something prehistoric about parrots ("antediluvian" was the term he used), and the way they walked reminded him of lizards, as though they had handed down across the generations an ancestral memory of the time before they had feathers.

Another of his parrots, Cotorrito, bit him only once, and Bowles blamed himself for the incident. Bowles had bought himself a new pair of shoes in Mexico City, and they made a squeaking sound when he walked. When he came into the darkened apartment, Cotorrito attacked him, thinking he was an intruder. This is by no means a comprehensive list of the birds Bowles became involved with. There were many more in his life, and later, when he moved to Morocco, he took up his habit of keeping parrots once again. Bowles simply could not do without the complicated friendship he had with these birds.

IRENE PEPPERBERG APPROACHES parrots in a different way. She is an adjunct associate professor of psychology at Brandeis University in Massachusetts and a research associate at Harvard known for her work on the cognitive capabilities of parrots and how they compare with those of people and other animals. For a long time, her work was personified in her bird Alex, an African grey she bought in 1977 at a pet shop in Chicago. Pepperberg was proud to call Alex the "smartest parrot in the world."

In nature, greys live in large groups and roam the rainforest in search of fruit, seeds, and nuts. Pepperberg proved that parrots, with their walnut-sized brains, are much more intelligent than previously thought (easily as intelligent as a two-year-old child), and she overturned many generally accepted assumptions about the birds. Greys are particularly gifted talkers, and they can carry on simple conversations with people, distinguish between colors and shapes, and master more than one hundred words. Over the course of thirty years, Pepperberg managed to teach her bird two hundred words, which he knew how to use appropriately.

Alex could not only identify the shape and color of an object, but also the material from which it was made—for example, he could say "four-corner-wood-square" provided that was exactly what he was shown. Before Alex died at the age of thirty-one from a heart attack brought on by hardening of the arteries, his last words to Pepperberg were, reportedly, "You be good, see you tomorrow. I love you." The *New York Times* reported news of his death in an article entitled "Alex Wanted a Cracker, but Did He Want One?", which reads like an obituary. Under the headline "America Is in Mourning," the British newspaper the *Guardian* noted that "to his supporters he was proof that the phrase 'bird brain' should be expunged from the dictionary." Pepperberg created a foundation in Alex's name to help support her research, which she continues with two new parrots: Griffin (born in 1995) and April (born in 2013). Neither, however, is as clever as Alex.

AIMÉE MORGANA WENT a step further working with parrots. After she saw Pepperberg and her parrot on television in 1997, she began to teach her five-month-old African grey, N'kisi (pronounced "Nikisi"), how to talk the way you would teach a small child. For example, when N'kisi said the word "water," Morgana pointed to a glass of water. When the parrot was five years old, he reportedly knew seven hundred words and could use them correctly. By 2002, Morgana had recorded seven thousand sentences spoken by N'kisi.

There came a time when Morgana and her husband thought the bird could pick up on their thoughts and intentions telepathically and was not just choosing words at random: "I was thinking of calling Rob, and picked up the phone to do so, and N'kisi said, 'Hi, Rob,' as I had the phone in my hand and was moving toward the Rolodex to look up his number." Another time, Morgana was dreaming that she was using her tape recorder, when the bird—who always slept next to her—said out loud, "You gotta push the button," at exactly the moment she did this in her dream. The parrot's interjection woke her immediately.

In a series of experiments that Morgana developed with Rupert Sheldrake, a researcher in the rarified field of parapsychology who has conducted a number of experiments on telepathy between pets and their owners, she and the parrot were assigned separate rooms on different floors in the same building about 55 feet (17 meters) apart from each other. The bird could neither see nor hear

her. Morgana proceeded to open 149 envelopes. She looked at the images they contained for two minutes at a time. Each image had something to do with nineteen key words that the parrot had mastered. She was also connected to the bird by a cordless baby monitor, and both of them were observed via video camera during the experiment. The words the parrot uttered during the experiments were recorded by three independent transcribers who could not see what was going on and the words were considered to be significant if they were recorded by two out of three of the transcribers. In seventy-one tests, N'kisi said one or more of the key words. In twenty-three cases, the word he uttered corresponded directly to the photograph. Amazingly enough, there were considerably more hits than there would have been if the results had been random—which would have generated only twelve hits. Morgana interpreted the results to mean that the parrot was reacting telepathically to her thoughts.

WE CAN THANK the documentary filmmaker Judy Irving for giving us a somewhat different view of the wide world of people and their parrots—or perhaps we should say of parrots and their people? Her documentary *The Wild Parrots of Telegraph Hill* explores the relationship between a one-time homeless street musician named Mark Bittner (to whom she is now married) and a flock of free-flying, red-green parrots in San Francisco (most of them cherry-headed conures). The parrots were either intentionally released into the wild or escaped—it is no longer possible to trace back the events that led them to take wing. While the question for Bittner was whether he could survive financially, the question for the parrots was whether they could survive in the big city.

For six years, from 1993 to 1999, Bittner looked after the flock in the San Francisco waterfront neighborhood. After he noticed the parrots in trees, he started to feed them, and soon they came every day, often five times a day, expecting meals from Bittner's hand.

Gradually he came to recognize the particular characteristics of each parrot and even gave them names. Then Bittner disappeared for two years. When he came back in 2001, he resumed feeding the birds, but this time only once a day. In his absence, the flock had considerably increased in size, and he no longer recognized individual birds. Now, thanks to the success of a book he wrote about the birds while Irving was working on her documentary, he can afford a better lifestyle and the parrots still come to him.

There are differing opinions about whether the birds really belong in San Francisco. They are not bothered by the relatively cold temperatures (in comparison with their tropical homeland). In San Francisco, their main threats are hawks and people who try to catch them and take them home with them—an act that is punishable by law. Feeding them in the parks is also strictly forbidden. Still, they thrive, and as the years go by, "the wild parrots of Telegraph Hill" are expanding their territory to other parts of the city.

THERE IS NO doubt that artists have a special affinity with pigeons and doves. It is well known that Pablo Picasso grew up surrounded by them. His father, whose nickname was El Palomero (the Pigeon Fancier), raised them, and they were ubiquitous in Malaga, Picasso's hometown. They perched in the sycamores around the Plaza de la Merced, where Pablo and his sisters used to play, and Pablo would use a stick to trace outlines of the birds in the dirt. Little Pablo was an inveterate sketcher, much to the dismay of his teachers. Once in a while, he would bring one of the birds to school and spend his time drawing his model instead of concentrating on his lessons. In 1949, a drawing Picasso had made of a fan-tailed pigeon given to him by his friend Henri Matisse was chosen for a poster for the First International Peace Conference in Paris. Picasso later reworked the image into a simple line sketch that became one of the world's most recognizable symbols of peace.

Some creative people—Frank Zappa, Walt Disney, Yul Brynner, and even the boxing legend Mike Tyson—are or have been known for breeding pigeons. And the Serbian-American inventor Nikola Tesla (1856–1943) was famous for feeding the pigeons in Central Park a special seed mix prepared by the chef at the Hotel New Yorker, where he rented an apartment. His rooms became a popular destination for pigeons he had rescued and nursed back to health. He said that he loved one beguiling white female as "a man loves a woman," and he was sure she loved him back. The bird's death was a great blow to a man who seemed more comfortable in the company of these birds than with people.

KEEPING PIGEONS IS a hobby that transcends the borders of countries and the coastlines of continents; in the Middle East, it stretches back thousands of years. In Fikirtepe, a modest neighborhood on Istanbul's Asian side, almost half the inhabitants breed

درین مظهر که انوار ظهور است اگر بینی تماشای حضور است

سیاغ بن رحم خویش به نگر کبوترهای را پرواز دور است

pigeons. Here, as in other regions of Turkey, people are particularly proud of the tumbling somersaults their pigeons execute to perfection. Many people in Iran also have a close relationship with pigeons, and the birds are almost everywhere in the villages that dot the countryside. Famous breeders such as Babak Arbab Khosro have devised codes of ethics for living with pigeons; in this part of the world, raising pigeons and the desire for self-improvement are inextricably intertwined. Those who own pigeons say that they love their birds. They breed them to select for beauty and stamina—for birds that can fly for up to eleven hours at a stretch and reach heights where they are no longer visible to the naked eye—and competitions to test the birds are held every August. Pigeon breeding has also long been a tradition in Egypt, where people soon noticed the birds' exceptional sense of direction and deployed them to disseminate information. Early European travelers to Egypt often did not know what to make of the distinctive clay pigeon houses—often cone-shaped with rounded tops—that towered above the other buildings in the cities. To this day, pigeons are bred in cities such as Mit Gahmr, where they are used as food and their droppings are a valuable fertilizer.

AT FIRST, CHARLES Darwin (1809–82) was not particularly interested in fancy pigeon breeding, which was a popular pastime for certain segments of the British population in his day. Naturalists then had a distinct aversion to, and you might even say contempt for, these birds and the people who kept them. However, after Darwin joined fancy pigeon societies and attended several pigeon shows, the genial scientist put the intellectual and societal divides of the times behind him. Darwin—who once wrote, "We cannot change the structure of a bird as quickly as we can the fashion of our dress"—realized that pigeons are cheap and easy to breed in confined spaces. Now that he was in direct contact with pigeon breeders, who cultivated close relationships with their birds, he could personally observe the selection process at work in domestically bred pigeons.

Darwin began his first serious research into domesticated pigeons in 1855. He constructed a pigeon house in his garden, bought birds in Fleet Street in London, and built up contacts with breeders who sent him birds from as far away as Persia and India. The multiplicity of pigeon breeds helped him refine his theory of evolution. He gained key insights into what he called "methodical" and "unconscious" choices—that is, intervention by the breeder in order to breed for a certain characteristic as opposed to the mostly invisible processes that all breeders set in motion when they purchase only the best birds and then crossbreed them. At the same time, he came closer to recognizing the important role played by differences between individual birds.

Darwin soon realized that all domesticated pigeons were descended from a single wild species, the rock dove, and he drew up a family tree in which he divided domesticated pigeons into four separate groups based on morphology. So much for Darwin, the scientist, but just how far did his emotional involvement with pigeons go? He is known to have told his friend and mentor Charles Lyell that pigeons were "the greatest treat, in my opinion, which can be offered to a human being"—quite a turnaround from his initial reaction to these birds and their owners.

THE BERLIN BIRD lover Adolf Walter had an unusual house pet: a long-eared owl, which he found in a deciduous wood in Brieselang near the Berlin suburb of Spandau on August 1, 1869.

The adult long-eared owl sitting on the nest looked straight at me with wide-open eyes as it stretched its head out of the nest, its tufted ear feathers sticking straight up. As soon as I touched the tree, however, it left the nest, which was stuck in a young birch tree only about twelve feet off the ground. It had likely previously been used as an aerie by a sparrowhawk. In the nest, which was within easy reach, there were four young long-eared owls of distinctly different sizes, although all were still sporting their downy feathers. The largest was the size of a turtle dove; the smallest hardly bigger than a house sparrow. The latter, which wasn't yet snapping its beak to warn me away like the others, was the one I took and kept in a cage for the next seventeen years.

The creature, which was as adorable as it was odd, was, as he had suspected, barely a week old. It exhibited no fear and grew quickly on a diet of wood mice and voles procured from the Berlin Zoo. Of most interest is Walter's description of the owl's demeanor.

Although it remained as trusting and unafraid with me and my wife as it had been before and it was not unfriendly with the servants, it was vicious with strangers. Around this time, Dr. Reichenow from the Berlin Museum visited me, and when I brought him into the room where the owl was, it immediately flew at his head and struck at his forehead with the talons of one foot, drawing blood. It then settled down on the stove without making any further attack.

Apart from such behavior, Walter praised the owl's "playful" nature. Apparently, what it enjoyed most was "tearing strips or balls of paper into little pieces."

The second year, Walter thought the owl was displaying some kind of courtship behavior with his wife:

Spring rolled around. Now, when my wife came into the neighboring room from outside and approached the owl's room, the bird immediately sprang from his perch down onto the ground. It immediately ran once around in a circle with its head held low and then hid behind a cigar box in its cage and crouched low to the ground as though it were a cat. If my wife did not enter and walked away from the door again, then it immediately stood up and came forward. But he slipped quickly back behind the box as soon as my wife's footsteps were clearly audible once again. When my wife opened the door, the owl would jump out from behind the box, stand in the middle of the bottom of the cage, stamp its feet, and hoot at her with a deep, slowly articulated "whoo-whoo-whoo," all the while inclining its head to the ground but keeping its eyes directed up at my wife. At the same time, he would beat his wings up and down.

This behavior went hand in hand with hostility toward Walter. Only after the beginning of summer did the owl show its gentler side once again. In the end, the bird succumbed to what was believed to be a stroke.

Walter could not have known that one day there would be so many books about living with an owl that they could be considered to be their own genre. There will probably be books about owls for as long as there are owls—or until the extremely dubious practice of keeping them as pets is completely outlawed, for they do not readily accept being handled and they certainly cannot be housetrained. They are really not suitable as pets at all, and CITES (the Convention on International Trade in Endangered Species of Wild Fauna and Flora, also known as the Washington Convention) allows them to be kept only under strict legally binding conditions.

PROBABLY THE BEST-KNOWN owl expert in the world is Heimo J. Mikkola of Finland. Over the course of four decades, his work for the United Nations has taken him to 128 countries, where he has seen about 120 species of owls. He could cover all 250 species that exist today in his book *Owls of the World* because he had owl watchers everywhere send him their photographs.

Mikkola has stories of many strange experiences he has had with owls, and they are a testament to how completely he blocked out the rest of his surroundings when he embarked on the trail of an owl. On the border of the then–Soviet Union, he once got into an altercation with guards when, while observing a Ural owl, he briefly stepped over the line to collect an owl pellet. And while he was looking for the Seychelles scops owl on the island of Mahé, he inadvertently wandered too close to the president's palace and was arrested on suspicion of being an assassin. However, he was able to convince the police that the guttural noises they heard mostly at night were not being made by frogs as they had thought (although the owls do feed on tree frogs) but by one of the rarest owls in the

½

world. He was released and allowed to resume his search with the president's blessing. The Seychelles scops owl was declared extinct in 1906, but was rediscovered in a mountain cloud forest fifty years later. Another close call came on an internal flight in South Africa. Mikkola had a southern white-faced owl along with him, and it escaped from its basket in the cabin. Luckily, the bird was quickly located, because in South Africa owls are thought to bring bad luck.

Mikkola, who calls himself an "owlaholic," has been observing birds since the age of eleven. He collects owl figurines, keeps live owls, and is a fan of owls when it comes to home security. He wrote that owls were "better guards than dogs," and that "nobody dared to enter our house alone due to owls."

OWLS AND BIRDS of prey are challenging birds to keep at home, as Helen Macdonald attests in her international bestseller *H Is for Hawk*. After the unexpected death of her father—a photographer who suffered a heart attack—she bought a female goshawk for eight hundred pounds sterling (about US$1,000) and obsessively devoted herself to taming the bird in her tiny apartment in Cambridge, England. She called the goshawk Mabel and recognized in the bird something she yearned for in herself: "The hawk was everything I wanted to be: solitary, self-possessed, free from grief and numb to the hurts of human life."

Macdonald's attempt to deal with her grief over the loss of her father is woven into her struggle to train her hawk and gain Mabel's trust. She was with the bird day and night, so close that she could make out the smell of "pepper and musk and burned stone" on her breath. After six months, Mabel was calm enough that she could safely be kept in an aviary for the duration of her molt, a time when she needed peace and quiet to replace her feathers. Macdonald was loath to leave her.

I put my hand out, drag the tips of my fingers down her tear-drop-splashed front. The new feathers she will grow will be barred stone-grey and white. The tones of earth and ochre will disappear. Her eyes, when I see her next, will be the deep orange of glowing coals.

The hawk was changing, as was Macdonald. In the fall, they would reconnect and start again—together.

MACDONALD'S STRUGGLE WITH her hawk has strange points of connection with the events in another book she weaves into her story: *The Goshawk* by T.H. White (1906–64). White retreated from thirty years of teaching in a boys' school (he is said to have defied the ban against hitting pupils) to a cottage in the country to devote himself to writing books and training a young goshawk he had ordered from Germany. His book, written in the style of a journal, tells of the ups and downs of his interactions with this bird. In order to break the bird's will, he deprived it of sleep, and in so doing brought himself to the brink of his own physical limits. The fact that he loved the bird and hated himself did not stop him from developing violent fantasies about his charge, which he sometimes called "Gos" and other times "Caligula" or "choleric beast." Driven by an impulse to exercise control over others, White inflicted on the bird the violence and neglect he himself had endured as a child. *The Goshawk* was never intended to be a book about how to train a hawk, as White was focused on his own experiences. He stuck with writing the story he wanted to write and cared not a jot for how professional falconers might judge his work.

THERE IS A particular thrill to taming birds that left to their own devices would simply fly away and ignore us completely, especially those with a fiercely wild and independent spirit, such as owls, falcons, and hawks. But bear in mind that keeping owls and birds of prey is forbidden in most countries or requires a special permit. This is easy to overlook when you get caught up in stories about people developing relationships with exotic wild birds and tales of their often charming antics. Some birds' last chance at survival may be in an aviary, but unless they are wounded or in critical danger, there are many arguments against keeping such birds in captivity unless you are an expert. Wild things belong in wild places.

{ 9 }

A Walk on the Wild Side

H OW IS IT that we find some birds fascinating and others move us not at all? Jeremy Mynott, author of *Birdscapes*, has tried to come up with general criteria to answer this question. He distinguishes between "beautiful" birds and "charismatic" birds. In his opinion, birds such as pheasants, Canada geese, and magpies may be beautiful, but they are not particularly charismatic. Barn owls, cranes, and red kites, however, are near the top of his list of charmers. Rarity can also be a reason birds attract attention. Then there are penguins—proof positive that beauty, charisma, and rarity are not the only characteristics that send bird enthusiasts into raptures. Penguins are appealing on so many levels: they do not look like a typical bird, their upright waddle positively invites us to imbue them with human characteristics, and, last but not least, they make us smile.

The first human contact with "penguins" was somewhat confusing. Initially the name described the great auk, a bird that has since gone extinct. Like penguins, the great auk was an upright, black-and-white, flightless bird, but it lived only in the North Atlantic and was not even remotely related to the birds we know as penguins today. Of the seventeen different species, the emperor and the Adélie embody the stereotypical penguin ideal, a tuxedoed caricature of a person that has mastered the art of walking upright more skillfully than *Homo sapiens*'s close relatives, the chimpanzees and gorillas. It was a theory about emperor penguin eggs that inspired Captain Scott's ill-fated 1911 British Antarctic Expedition. Up until this time, the emperor penguin had been considered to be the most primitive bird on Earth. It was hoped that by studying the development of the embryo in the egg, scientists could discover not only the complete evolutionary history and origin of birds, but also their relationship to other vertebrates.

The story of the emperor penguin—one of three species of penguin that live only in Antarctica and its immediate vicinity—and its relationship with modern humans is the story of the most intriguing love affair ever between people and birds. Hardly any other bird (with the exception of owls, of which there are many different species spread across the world) provokes such a strong emotional response. Indeed, it may be the most beloved bird of all time, even though there is no single person who stands out as the archetypal "penguin nerd." Quite simply, too many people feel this way about penguins.

Naturally, only a limited number of people are able to spend much time observing penguins in their natural environment. Watching thousands of birds walking across isolated, ice-covered wastelands is a privilege restricted to specialized researchers and a wealthy class of tourist, which is probably the main reason the penguin has entered the general consciousness as an almost mythical creature. In the French Oscar-winning documentary film *March of the Penguins* by Luc Jacquet (*La marche de l'empereur*, 2005), the life of the emperor penguin is presented as a parable for survival in a hostile environment. Fundamentalist Christians soon laid claim to the film and its message—above all because they embraced the penguins' behavior as a shining example of monogamy and thought their existence confirmed the theory of "intelligent design." It strained credulity, they argued, to think that natural selection could ever have produced a bird that lived such an austere and challenging lifestyle. Adopting the penguins as mascots for their belief system inevitably sparked a heated debate.

In his 2007 documentary movie *Encounters at the End of the World*, Werner Herzog interviewed scientists at the McMurdo Station in Antarctica, including penguin researcher David G. Ainley, who has been researching the connection between the size of penguin colonies and changes in the climate for nigh on twenty years.

> *It's rather unsettling to see them searching for rocks to raise their nests higher and higher to keep their eggs from floating away. Actually, pretty disgusting, knowing that it's we humans who have made their lives even more complex and tenuous.*

In one of the most moving scenes in the film, an Adélie penguin distances itself from the other birds in its colony and feeding stations at the edge of the ice for no apparent reason. It is later seen walking farther inland in the direction of a mountain chain. When the bird was caught and brought back to the feeding station, it immediately set off once again in the same direction. It was facing 3,000 miles (5,000 kilometers) of Antarctica and walking not only into complete isolation but also toward certain death.

RAVENS AND CROWS are the bad boys of the bird world. These raucous birds all dressed up in black just do not conform to our much-loved image of gentle, peaceable winged creatures. Gifted with extraordinary investigative skills, they are famous for exploiting every conceivable source of food. They have a reputation as merciless nest robbers, and grain farmers dislike them because they believe they lay waste to their fields. These distinctly different birds (same genus, different species) are tarred with the same brush. So, how to tell them apart? Ravens are larger with chunky beaks, a small beard of feathers on their throats, and wedge-shaped tails. Less enamored with urban life than crows, they shun cities and prefer less populated areas such as woodlands or even deserts.

John Marzluff, a biologist and professor at the University of Washington in Seattle, says that these birds are his favorite research subjects. He underscores the exceptional intelligence of crows and ravens, which has earned them the name "feathered apes." Apart from magpies, they are the only species of birds to recognize their own reflections in a mirror (the only other animals to do so are dolphins, elephants, and the great apes), meaning they have at least a basic level of self-awareness. Marzluff writes:

Crows are super smart because they have long lifespans, spend considerable portions of their lives with others in social groups, and learn quickly through trial and error and by observation. Their brains, like our own, allow crows to form lasting, emotionally charged memories. They dream and reconsider what they see and hear before acting.

Marzluff's observations laid the groundwork for a new understanding of how people and corvids have coexisted for thousands of years and how in comparison with crows, ravens have gradually retreated and oftentimes even been ousted by crows. He sees nothing less than a symbiotic relationship at work, which continues thanks to the birds' highly developed ability to adapt to new surroundings and new sources of food, which, in turn pushes the birds to come up with new ways to exploit them. Marzluff backs up his theories with fascinating examples. Carrion crows in Sendai, Japan, for example, take walnuts they gather in the fall and carefully place them in front of cars stopped at red lights so that the cars crack the shells when they drive off and the birds can then consume the nuts inside. A recent Japanese study has shown that crows are capable of making connections between symbols on containers and their contents. When it comes to questions about which birds are the most intelligent, it seems corvids can compete with parrots.

THERE ARE OTHER species of birds that we can only really begin to understand when they are free to live in their natural environments. These include the thirteen species of finches that inhabit the volcanic Galápagos Islands. The main difference between them is the shape of their beaks. Some of them have beaks that look like the beaks of grosbeaks or small parrots; others have beaks that are so small that they resemble the beaks of warblers. There are noticeable behavioral differences, as well. The woodpecker finch is one fascinating example. It manages to extract larvae out of small cavities with the help of a twig or cactus spine, a skill it has obviously developed on account of its very short tongue. Then there is the sharp-beaked ground finch, which sucks the blood of other birds, earning it the nickname "vampire finch." These details escaped Charles Darwin, who spent about a month on four of the islands as part of his voyage on the *Beagle* in 1835. Surprisingly, Darwin did not say a word about the finches he found in the Galápagos when he wrote *On the Origin of Species*. Despite this omission, his visit to the Galápagos definitely triggered the development of his theory of evolution, even though at the time Darwin was more interested in the geology of the islands and collecting plant samples for his friend and mentor John Stevens Harlow. The real significance of the finches seemed to dawn on him only after a meeting with John Gould a year and a half later, when Gould confirmed that there really were thirteen different species, they were all closely related, and they lived nowhere else in the world.

More than one hundred years after he encountered them, Darwin's finches garnered considerable attention among ornithologists. In 1938, the British evolutionary biologist David Lack (1910–63) visited the Galápagos. Before this journey, he had been busy with, among other things, the knotty problem of measuring the life spans of European robins, a study that resulted in *The Life of the Robin*. On his return from the islands, he wrote another book: *Darwin's Finches*. Lack came to the astounding realization that in no other bird are the species so sharply delineated from each other as they are on these islands. Since Lack published his observations in 1947, the finches have been routinely associated with Darwin's name.

Current thinking divides the thirteen species of finches into four groups whose members are particularly closely related. The birds in the first group live in trees and feed on fruit and beetles; those in the second are completely vegetarian. Those in the third group also live in trees, but snatch insects out of the air as warblers do, hence their common names: green and gray warbler-finches. Those in the fourth group, which comprises six different species and is therefore the largest, live strictly on the ground. The delineations between each species are complicated by the fact that the shapes and sizes of beaks within each species can be very different.

Peter and Rosemary Grant have been observing the finches on Daphne Major Island since 1973, following finch evolution in real time. Their observations are made easier by the fact that the finches are not in the least bit shy.

> *When we walk up to them, the birds keep doing what they are doing; but when an owl comes near, they head for a cactus tree. A little while ago, Rosemary was crossing a treeless spot. An owl flew over, and finches flew up from all around and landed on Rosemary!*

In 1981, the Grants found a ground finch that, weighing in at just about 1 ounce (30 grams), was almost one-fifth of an ounce (at least 5 grams) heavier than all the other finches they had studied to date. Genetic analysis showed that it had probably come over from neighboring Santa Cruz Island. They gave it the number 5110 and followed the development of its descendants for seven generations. And there were indeed differences between them and the other ground finches, most markedly in beak shape and song. It is well known that beak shape is an important element in mate choice; however, the Grants believe it highly unlikely that the descendants of this finch will remain isolated long enough to generate a completely new species.

FROM OCTOBER 1940 to August 1941, I had the opportunity to get to know the area around Auschwitz and to take particular note of

the birds that lived there. In the fall and winter months and early
spring my duties with the Waffen-SS left me with little time for
birdwatching.

A bad joke? How does the idyllic world of birds intersect with the
horrors of Auschwitz? What at first reads like an absurdist sketch
is actually a document written by Günther Niethammer (1908–
74), who wrote his doctoral thesis on the development of crops in
birds and did indeed study the birds around this most horrifying
of places. Furthermore, he clearly did so in an official capacity, for
after he had served as a camp guard for two years, he was assigned
to special ornithological tasks in the area.

Niethammer clearly preferred studying a small area intensively to giving a larger area a more superficial investigation, and he recorded the different species of birds he observed with great precision.

> *Magpies are particularly prevalent here. They have found their way into all the villages and have become targets for small-game hunters. For the most part the meadows are very damp, and there you can find redshanks, lapwings, and wagtails, all typical for this type of landscape. In dry fields overrun by weeds, you can also find quail, although not very many of them.*

He continues with a comparison with other regions in Germany and concludes that the lack of some bird species around Auschwitz can be readily explained by its geographical location. He also finds the huge flocks of starlings noteworthy. "Observations on the Birds of Auschwitz," an essay he published in 1941, is illustrated with idyllic images of the Sola River, which flows within yards of the camp.

THE SWISS ORNITHOLOGIST Hans Arn (1907–72) specialized in nature in urban settings. For over four decades he devoted himself to the study of alpine swifts, which could be found in large numbers in his beautiful baroque home town of Solothurn. Arn gathered his data at just two locations: the Jesuit church and Biel Gate, one of the original entrances to the city. He was in contact with David Lack, who had moved on from Darwin's finches to study Eurasian swifts.

Arn devoted some space in his book *Biologische Studien am Alpensegler* (Biological Studies of the Alpine Swift) to the question of whether aerial mating "could be an active or successful sexual act" or whether it was only a question of "paired flight that looked like copulation." In his own words:

When Lack saw a copulation with me on May 28, 1954, at the Jesuit church at 06:40 on the wall by the landing site in Field 20, we stayed for another hour on the tower of St. Ursen's church. Even though many alpine swifts and common swifts were hunting and playing over the town and we could hear the whispering noises leading up to the act of pairing, we did not observe any acts of mating on the wing.

One year later, he observed two pairs that were "very loving with one another." He wrote that "they were definitely 'cuddling,' pressing up against one another or ruffling each other's neck feathers, billing and making soft, whispering sounds, but there was no copulation."

Arn missed the act itself, for one week later, on June 5, 1955, the first egg appeared in the nest. And then there was another surprise.

The same day, I was watching the alpine swifts flying up to the Biel Gate when at 18:10 I heard characteristic mating calls and observed an aerial copulation no more than 30 meters away… The birds' behavior and position during this paired flight, which lasted only a few seconds, suggested that it was a case of successful copulation. The female flew in a straight line, the male alighted onto the female's back from above, the two cloacas made contact, and shortly thereafter the male took off from the female's back. During the act of copulation, the pair flew together for a distance of about 10 meters.

Arn also often mulled over the question of whether alpine swifts can sleep on the wing. Thanks to later experiments in which birds were fitted with transmitters and sensors to monitor their physical functions, scientists now know that they certainly can do that, although they may reduce the rate at which they beat their wings while they are sleeping. And indeed they must be able to sleep on the wing, because they can remain airborne for up to two hundred days at a stretch. In the fall, they fly non-stop from the Alps to Africa, a distance of over 1,800 miles (3,000 kilometers), and no roosting sites have ever been found in their winter quarters.

OBSERVING BIRDS WITHOUT interfering with their lives seems to me to be the purest form of getting to know them. Flight is one of the most breathtaking bird behaviors to watch, and the fastest and most fearless of fliers is the peregrine falcon. The elusive Englishman John Alec Baker (1926–86) must be one of the most passionate observers of peregrine falcons ever. In his book *The Peregrine,* he remembers the first peregrine he saw.

> *I have seen many since then, but none has excelled it for speed and fire of spirit. For ten years I spent all my winters for that restless brilliance, for the sudden passion and violence that peregrines flush from the sky.*

The peregrines Baker observed flew from Scandinavia to the British Isles in the fall, following the birds they hunted: plovers, lapwings, thrushes, and starlings. Baker's book takes the form of a winter journal. He roams the Essex countryside in rubber boots, spotting scope in hand, crossing fens, fields, woods, and gardens, no matter the weather. As far as we can tell, his records probably started in 1963, the time when the use of pesticides, above all DDT, was depleting the population of these birds to such an extent that they were threatened with extinction.

Baker reacted to the unbridled passion he saw in peregrines—birds that almost always catch and kill their prey on the wing. And he spared no details in describing the bloody process. The birds can drop like a stone out of the sky or shoot up into the air to catch their prey from below. Baker wanted nothing more fervently than to be able to fly with them, to become one with them. And in a way he achieved his wish—at least in his vivid portrayal of their lives.

Little is known about Baker's own life. Even though he preferred to undertake his bird-watching expeditions by bicycle, he worked for a time as a manager for the British Automobile Association and later for a manufacturer of fruit juices. He suffered from debilitating rheumatoid arthritis and took strong painkillers to ease his chronic pain. Despite his relative youth, he was often confined to bed, where he turned his bird-watching notes into soaring prose:

> *Crisp and golden in the sunlight, [the peregrine] swam up though the warm air with muscular undulations of his wings, like the waving flicker of a fish's fins. He drifted on the surface, a tiny silver flake on the blue burnish of the sky. His wings tightened and bent back, and he slid away to the east, a dark blade cutting slowly through blue ice. Moving down through sunlight, he changed colour like an autumn leaf, passing from shining gold to pallid yellow, turning from tawny to brown, suddenly flicking out black against the skyline.*

{ 10 }

Is Bird Love a One-Way Street?

A S BOLD AS Hans Arn's speculations were about the love lives of alpine swifts, and as impassioned as J.A. Baker was in pursuit of his peregrines, their observations bring up a much more provocative question: Are birds capable of true attachments to people? Can birds be "mad for" people? Ludwig Büchner (1824–99) was a German doctor and naturalist who saw the principles of love expressed everywhere in the world, even at the atomic level. In his book *Liebe und Liebes-Leben in der Thierwelt* (Love and Love Lives in the Animal World), he claimed that even the "wild, freedom-loving nature" of birds of prey "does not keep them from forming friendships with people and devoting their love to them." He based his view on accounts from people such as the German pastor Christian Ludwig Brehm (1787–1864), who reported that the eagle in the zoo he liked to visit every day greeted him "with a friendly call" as soon as the bird caught sight of him. Büchner wrote that the relationship between people and caged birds was even more intimate. For many people, "the friendship and attachment of their birds is a constant and indispensable source of enjoyment and entertainment, and their interactions with their birds are often on a par with the interactions they have with other people."

It is remarkable how quickly people draw conclusions about the emotional life of birds, as though they really can understand them. They clearly assume they share some kind of spiritual kinship. Büchner documented the case of the Italian ornithologist Paulo Savi, who possessed an alpine chough "with a very sweet disposition." This bird "enjoyed complete freedom, but it never took advantage of this to fly away. On the contrary, it used its freedom to constantly give its master, whom it loved so tenderly, new proofs of its love and affection." And then there is the tame moorhen belonging to a Doctor Fasolt from Saalfeld that

> stuck to him like a shadow whenever he was at home. When he wrote, ate, or drank coffee, the bird sat close to him on his desk. If he went into another room, the bird accompanied him. When he lay down at night, the bird crept under the covers with only its head sticking out so it could breathe.

Christian Brehm's son Alfred Edmund Brehm (1829–84) was apparently on the same wavelength as Büchner. In his book *Leben der Vögel* (The Lives of Birds), he confidently recorded that Count Gourcy-Droitaumont's two rock thrushes broke out into a particular song every time he came home "in order to please him." And he offered the intriguing idea that the birds had embraced the role of domestic police.

> When one of the two hundred caged birds the count possessed escaped without the count noticing, all the rest made an awful noise to indicate that something untoward had happened and didn't quiet down until the fugitive had been returned.

He also gave a dramatic example of the apparent love and tenderness of a bullfinch. When his master traveled, the bird became very sad, but when he came home, he was full of joy: "He flapped his wings, nodded greetings, sang his master's favorite songs, fluttered up and down in the cage, and was then suddenly silent and fell off his perch—dead."

And yet—and one could take this as an argument in favor of Büchner and Brehm's thesis, which at first blush might appear somewhat strange—it is known that parrots often do not survive the death of their owners if that person has owned them for a long time. The most famous case is that of a gray parrot belonging to Frances Stewart, mistress of the English king Charles II. She owned her parrot for over forty years and it outlived her by only four days.

IT IS NOT only parrots that appear capable of the kind of devotion that you only expect to encounter in human relationships. Ambrose G.H. Pratt (1874–1944) has left us a beautiful example and record of just such a relationship between a human being and a bird. A superb lyrebird plays a lead role. The superb lyrebird is native to eastern Australia and its neighboring island, Tasmania, and is one of two representatives of the genus *Menura*, which is Greek for "moon tail." The name refers to the translucent crescent moon shapes that decorate the ends of the birds' tail feathers. The superb lyrebird is an unusual-looking bird, a bit like a cross between a pheasant and a peacock. It has long been said that its primary tail plumes—they can be up to 2 feet (60 centimeters) long—form the shape of a lyre or small U-shaped harp, although the tail as a whole actually looks more like a fan or sometimes—when the bird thrusts it forward to cover its head—even like a bridal veil.

What is most unusual about the superb lyrebird is its vocal skills. More than three-quarters of the sounds it makes are based on mimicry, and it has an exceptional repertoire. It can mimic the calls of neighboring birds, the peeping noises made by nestlings being fed, the rustle of parrot feathers, the croaking of frogs, the barks and howls of dogs, the yipping of foxes, the cries of possums fighting one another, or a stuck pig. Some people claim to have recognized the sounds of car engines (apparently even different makes such as Porsches or Ferraris), gun shots, axe blows, chainsaws, and the crackling of bush fires. Pratt wrote with admiration, "One of the most beautiful and rare and probably the most intelligent of all the world's wild creatures is that incomparable artist, the Lyrebird *(Menura novae-hollandiae)*."

As he was investigating the "mindset" of the bird, he observed play between neighboring cocks.

The favourite game is very like the childish (human) game of "follow-my-leader." The birds will chase each other over rocks and under logs and around trees and stumps, clucking musically, and apparently delighting in the exercise, for several minutes... The entire game is conducted in the most friendly spirit, and it never leads to or ends in any sort of quarrelling.

He praised the birds' domestic arrangements, as well: "The domestic life of the Menura is extraordinarily placid and affectionate. The functions of husband and wife are clearly defined and are accepted as inevitable obligations and discharged by either without contest or quarrelling."

And female lyrebirds are, apparently, exceedingly appreciative of their mate's dancing prowess: "[T]he hen bird never tires of the male's performances, but always provides him with an attentive and apparently insatiable audience."

He also noticed that lyrebirds seem to have a particular love of beauty, which they express not only in their mating displays, but also in their choice of tree on which to perch: "His favourite is the blackwood, whose dark, umbrageous foliage and graceful form marks it out as one of the most charming of Australia's forest growths."

The birds seem to appreciate fragrance, as well. According to Pratt, they haunt stands of sweet-smelling musk and sassafras, perhaps because they have developed a keen sense of smell to warn them of the approach of odiferous predators such as wild cats and foxes. A happy lyrebird, it seems, likes to sing its song surrounded by "enchanting perfumes."

The most amazing thing about the lyrebird in Pratt's book was its relationship with a woman called Mrs. Wilkinson, who lived in hermit-like isolation. Mrs. Wilkinson lived near a remote mountain valley that she had preserved for wildlife. Her business was growing cut flowers for the Melbourne market. One morning, to her great astonishment, a male lyrebird appeared in front of her house, calmly pecking for grubs. Lyrebirds are by nature extremely shy and are rarely seen, so Mrs. Wilkinson felt honored by the visit. As their relationship progressed, she built the bird a platform outside her sitting room window where he could display and sing, and, with the exception of one time when she couldn't help herself and reached out to touch him, she was careful never to intrude upon his personal space. In return, he kept her company, and for the time of year when he was in possession of his magnificent tail feathers, he entertained her with song. Once he dropped his tail feathers in August, however, he retreated to the forest as though ashamed that he had lost his finery. He profited from his seclusion by expanding his vocal repertoire and returned in the fall to proudly display to his human companion not only his newly grown tail feathers but also his latest songs.

Mrs. Wilkinson and the bird, which she called James, appeared to have a close, almost telepathic relationship—according to Pratt's account, at least. On one occasion, Mrs. Wilkinson was taken ill and had to retire to bed.

Nausea beset her, and for several hours she lay prostrate, wondering in the intervals between spasms of acute sickness how long a time must pass before some tradesmen or neighbours might come to whom she could appeal for help. She fell at length into an exhausted slumber, to be awakened by strange scratching sounds outside her bedroom window. They continued for at least an hour, then suddenly the head of her beloved bird appeared in silhouette above the sill, and "James" began to sing to her as she had never heard him sing before. The lovely miracle cured Mrs. Wilkinson more effectively than could all the physicians in the capital.

On another occasion, Mrs. Wilkinson left home for a couple of weeks to visit a sick relative. When she got back, the caretaker told her that James had not visited the house in all the time that she had been away. She said she was not worried because she had told the bird she would be gone for a fortnight. "He will come to see me to-morrow," she declared. It turned out she did not even have to wait that long: "That very evening, while she was preparing tea, the bird appeared on his platform and clamorously demanded her attention."

Thanks to Pratt's book, lyrebirds have a special place in the story of people who love birds and the birds who love them back.

"THE MARVEL OF a hummingbird's egg transcends the wonders of the Milky Way." The man who wrote these words, the French historian Jules Michelet (1798–1874), is a man whose love for birds was extraordinary even when measured by the standards of the bird-obsessed. In *The Bird*, his first book on the philosophy of Nature (or, as we would call it today, natural science), he investigated not only the egg, but also the bird in and of itself. In this book, Michelet demonstrates a love for all birds in language that soars into hyperbole. The depressing notion that "human carelessness" harms birds pervades the pages. He becomes upset about the plight of a nightingale confined to a cage, a treatment he finds cruel and inhumane—so much so that it pains him to hear the tortured and downcast creature's song.

When he wrote about birds, Michelet expressed himself freely and did not worry about expert opinion. Here are just a couple of examples from a book filled with richly detailed bird portraits. This is his unusual yet illuminating take on the penguin:

> *The stiffness of their small arms—one can scarcely call them wings in these rudimentary birds—their awkwardness on land, their difficulty of movement, prove that they belong to the ocean, where they swim with wonderful ease, and which is their natural and legitimate element. One might speak of them as its emancipated eldest sons, as ambitious fishes, candidates for the characters of birds, which had already progressed so far as to transform their fins into scaly pinions.*

For the ostrich, he came up with an equally thought-provoking analogy. He called it "the navigator of the desert" and described it as a "bird camel"

> *resembling the camel itself in its internal structure. At least, if its imperfect wings cannot raise it above the earth, they assist it powerfully in walking and endow it with extraordinary swiftness: it is the sail with which it skims its arid African ocean.*

For Michelet, birds abound where people fear to tread. He can be seen as the Walt Whitman of natural philosophy.

> *Melodious sparks of celestial fire, whither do ye not attain? For ye exists not height nor distance; the heaven, the abyss, it is all one. What cloud, what watery deep is inaccessible to ye! Earth, in all its*

vast circuit, great as it is with its mountains, its seas, and its valleys, is wholly yours. I hear ye under the Equator, ardent as the arrows of the sun. I hear ye at the Pole, in the eternal lifeless silence, where the last tuft of moss has faded; the very bear sees ye afar, and slinks away growling. Yet, ye still remain; ye live, ye love, ye bear witness to God, ye reanimate death. In those terrestrial deserts your touching loves invest with an atmosphere of innocence what man has designated the barbarism of nature.

To Kill or Not to Kill?

THE NONCHALANCE WITH which exotic birds were dispatched up until the twentieth century is terrifying, even if it is understandable in the context of the times. Once the birds had been killed, preserving them became a race against time, as so aptly described by a ship's doctor named Franz Johann Friedrich Meyen (1804–40), who circumnavigated the world on the sailing ship *Luise* in 1830–32.

> *The northern provinces of Chile and the high plateaus of Peru could have yielded hundreds of species to enrich and adorn our collections. Every day, the most beautiful birds were shot and every night they had to be discarded when, as was usually the case, there was not sufficient time to preserve them all… In other places, such as the island of Manila, our collection attracted thousands and hundreds of thousands of ants, cockroaches, lizards, and other vermin that, in the course of a few hours, consumed the birds we thought we had safely stored.*

Up until the sixteenth century, hardly anyone gave much thought to how, or even whether, bird carcasses could be preserved so that they did not quickly succumb to the depredations of moths and other undesirables. But in order to study them in more detail or add them as eye-catching adornments to natural history collections, collectors had to come up with something.

The famous Dutch apothecary and collector Albert Seba (1665–1736) preserved many of his birds in alcohol, and Frederik Ruysch (1638–1731), a Dutch botanist and anatomist, dried his specimens and stashed each in a wide-necked bottle that he made airtight by stoppering it with a fish bladder secured with red silk. The French naturalist René-Antoine Ferchault de Rémur (1683–1757), who once complained that it was not possible to have a complete collection of birds because of "voracious insects," solved the problem by using the residual heat in a bread oven to carefully dry his skins and amassed what was the largest collection of birds in Europe in his day. It also soon got around that skins kept better when they were treated with arsenic. Countless people probably paid with their lives after innocently sprinkling this toxic substance over their collections.

IN THÜRINGEN, HIS theological career clearly left Christian Brehm with plenty of time to pursue his interest in birds. Brehm laid the foundation for his bird collection while he was still in high school. He was extremely methodical, collecting birds in their juvenile, breeding, and post-molt plumage. This attention to detail meant that his collection soon eclipsed those of his contemporaries. He honed his ability to detect details in bird morphology and plumage patterns, and in the birds' dependence on their environment. He attempted to understand everything about birds, including what they ate and how they reproduced. He noted the connection between climate and plumage: "Northern birds are covered with copious amounts of feathers. Indeed ptarmigan from Iceland and

Greenland have such a thick, dense coat in winter that it comes down right over their feet."

In his book *Beiträge zur Vogelkunde* (Contributions to Ornithology), Brehm described in detail the plumage, internal anatomy, and habits of 104 birds found in Germany. The parsonage with all Brehm's stuffed and living feathered companions was not only a private research center; it also developed into a mecca for bird aficionados and researchers from Germany and abroad, who found here practical advice, suggestions, opinions, and reference materials that could be found nowhere else. With *Ornis, oder das Neueste und Wichtigste der Vögelkunde* (Ornis, or the Latest and Most Important News in Ornithology), Brehm founded the first ornithological magazine in the world. He also published the *Handbuch der Naturgeschichte aller Vögel Deutschlands* (Handbook for the Natural History of All the Birds in Germany) and a separate handbook for those who kept tame birds. Bird collecting was a lifelong passion for him—almost disturbingly so. "I have owned hobbies [small Eurasian falcons] and kestrels, common buzzards and honey buzzards, long-eared owls, barn owls, tawny owls, and little owls," he wrote, "all of which were unusually tame, and they all knew and loved me." The very first bird in his collection is thought to have been a collared flycatcher in 1804, and he added the last specimen to his collection just a couple of months before he died sixty years later.

Over the course of half a century, the "bird pastor," as he was called, amassed an enormous collection of birds, which meant he was always wrestling with the problem of housing them all. Later he benefited from his son's travels, which exacerbated his problem. He tried unsuccessfully to interest the zoological museum in Berlin in his collection. It was only after the pastor's death and that of his son that the collection ended up in the hands of Lord Walter Rothschild, and from there it found its way to the American Museum of Natural History in New York in 1931. In the early 1960s, one-third of the contents were transferred to the Alexander Koenig Research Museum in Bonn.

BREHM'S SON ALFRED used to stand in front of his father's bird cages when he was just a young boy, transfixed by the wonder of it all. He also accompanied his father when he went out stalking birds in the Thuringian Forest (almost the entire forest was declared a nature park in 1990). Even before he attended university, he accompanied his brother, Oskar, to Egypt and Nubia (an area along the Nile encompassing modern-day northern Sudan to southern Egypt).

Birds made a deep impression on him, and Brehm gave free rein to his emotions and opinions when he wrote about them (or about any other animal, for that matter). In his book *Das Leben der Vögel* (The Lives of Birds), completely ignoring contemporary schools of thought, he divided birds very loosely into "crackers," "catchers," "spotters," and "swimmers." He certainly credited birds with intelligence, and he fully embraced the anthropomorphism rampant at the time and ascribed to them full-blown human emotions such as "pride," "hate," "love," and "gratitude." He also wrote of birds that were "happy, sad, boring, social, and reclusive... good-natured and irascible." He labeled some "lovable" and others "unlovable." He described nocturnal birds as "more sad than happy," "more grumpy than gay." He even named one species—the Thekla lark or *Galerita theklae*—after his only sister, who died young and—unlikely though it sounds—apparently never showed any particular interest in birds.

When Brehm's text was used as the basis for the English publication *Cassell's Book of Birds*, the editor lauded Brehm and wrote that he imparted "a freshness to his descriptions as characteristic of the real naturalist as the smell of new-made hay is redolent of fields and hedgerows."

Christian Ludwig Brehm

MARTHA D. MAXWELL (1831–81) is one of the least known of the Americans who stalked and collected birds in the nineteenth century. She was born in Pennsylvania and arrived in the West on the coattails of the gold rush in 1860. In 1874, she opened her Rocky Mountain Museum in Boulder (and later moved it to Denver). She also mounted exhibits in Philadelphia as part of the Centennial International Exhibition of 1876, the first official World's Fair held in the United States. Among the animals she displayed were hundreds of birds. Maxwell was reported to be a vegetarian.

BIRD HUNTERS WERE active in many other parts of the world, because the bird trade was a lucrative business. Often whole armies of hunters went out stalking. In Eastern Europe, the Dobruja, which lies between the Danube and the Black Sea, was a popular area for catching birds, and many activities that revolved around bird collecting were concentrated there: whole villages were busy year round working as hunters and climbers for the bird collectors.

This is how the trader Max Sintenis described the scene in 1877 for the *Journal für Ornithologie* (Journal of Ornithology):

> *In general, the Dobruja can still be regarded as an El Dorado for orni-thologists. However, the abundance of birds is diminishing markedly from year to year. The Turks have no hunting laws or if they do, they are laws in name only. Hunters of pelicans, swans, egrets, and loons [divers], greedy for plunder, ruthlessly run riot over the breeding grounds of their hapless victims. Gulls, terns, avocets, and ducks are all mercilessly robbed on account of their delicious eggs.*

IS IT POSSIBLE to love something and want to kill it at the same time? The contradiction between the desire to hunt and the desire

to conserve—and the tension this gives rise to—is a thread that runs through many ornithological biographies as attitudes started changing in the early part of the twentieth century.

The change is illustrated in the lives of researchers such as Hugo Weigold (1876–1973). Weigold was a marine biologist turned ornithologist who studied bird migration. He was a pioneer of bird banding and founder of the ornithological observatory on the German archipelago Heligoland, an isolated rocky outpost in the North Sea that later played a major role in German naval operations in World War I. He also coined the term "oil spill" and was one of the early campaigners in the bird conservation movement.

All of this is hard to believe when you consider the record he kept of his life. Take, for example, a long section devoted to his travels through northwestern Mesopotamia and the interior of Syria. From western Asia Minor, he reached Beirut via Cyprus, before continuing north. Weigold's travelogue is full of cold-blooded arrogance and tales of derring-do. In the course of retelling his journey, one scenario crops up over and over again: a completely idyllic situation ends abruptly in a bloodbath, which he describes with downright devilish glee. You can almost see him rubbing his hands together as he tells the tale. Sometimes an impulse holds him back initially, as happened on an island in the Euphrates where twenty hermit ibis were running around "like turkeys." He wrote regretfully, "How I longed to blast away at them. But a crowd of Arabs were hanging around and not of the best sort! And natives there consider the ibis to be a sacred bird."

Weigold targeted the birds later, despite the menacing locals, and blamed the birds' hard, tough feathers for his failure to kill a single one. He described a sparrowhawk hunting small birds in a nearby tree as flying "cockily" right past the barrel of his gun, as though the bird's disregard for his superiority was justification enough for killing it. At another stop, near the Turkish town of Urfa, he made no attempt to restrain himself from shooting birds in the gardens surrounding a mosque.

When Weigold had an enforced stopover in Lebanon while suffering from a severe case of food poisoning—and clearly under the influence of heavy doses of opium—he caught wind of extensive assaults on the local songbird population. He was, somewhat surprisingly, incensed.

> *Here, you would expect the gardens to reverberate with sweet bird-song. Instead, there's a bang here, a bang there, and one blackcap after another falls and is stuck through the neck with a sharpened twig until the unscrupulous bird murderer has collected a generous bundle.*

He claimed the beautiful landscape was being "desecrated" by barbaric hunters. Sickened by the sights and sounds of slaughter, he didn't even try to kill anything: "We shot not a single bird. We were fuelled by only one wish: to leave this murderous hole as soon as we possibly could."

His journey to China and Tibet, initially conceived as a two-year voyage, was drawn out into a six-year stay as a result of World War I. He left six thousand skins behind for ornithologists to study.

ORNITHOLOGICAL CHRONICLES OFFER a wealth of examples of other people who also reconciled the seemingly irreconcilable: hunting and conservation. The Benedictine priest Blasius Hanf (1808–92) made an inventory of 237 species of birds at Furtner Lake in Styria, Austria, which lies at an elevation of 2,850 feet (870 meters). Over the decades, Hanf shot more than one thousand birds there. As he once wrote in a letter to amateur naturalist Carl Andreas Naumann, he resorted to using "pipe tobacco to preserve the birds" after arsenic almost cost him his life on two separate occasions. These preserved specimens, along with more than a thousand others, were exhibited at the World Exposition held in Vienna in 1873. They can be found today at the monastery of St. Lambrecht, which in an ignominious episode in its history served as a satellite camp for Dachau (albeit at a time when monks were not in residence). Hanf also wrote a handful of articles on such subjects as dotterels (a small wader in the plover family), ptarmigans, crossbills, and cuckoos.

MEANWHILE, ACROSS THE ocean in the United States, Frank M. Chapman (1864–1945) was growing up in a well-to-do family of bankers and lawyers. He started out following in their footsteps until he heard about the fascinating ornithological discoveries a friend of his had made in the Amazon. In a trice, Chapman ditched his promising career in finance: he had been bitten hard by the bird bug. A few years later, he found himself once again in the company of the bird-obsessed. This time it was a group on the trail of the green-, yellow-, red-, and orange-colored Carolina parakeet in Florida, where the last of a population that had once been spread across the southeastern states had taken refuge. This was, incidentally, the only species of parrot on American soil, and by the end of the nineteenth century, its numbers had dwindled to a dangerously low level, because of both deforestation and persecution by farmers. It was precisely the bird's rarity that drew enthusiasts to move heaven and earth in order to capture the last living examples of the species. After two years of searching, Chapman finally found his birds in March 1889. He killed fifteen of them. Barely thirty years later, the last Carolina parakeet died in the Cincinnati Zoo. It is cold comfort to know that an estimated eight hundred skins, skeletons, and eggs from these birds are gathering dust in the cabinets of natural history museums around the world. For the next fifty years, Chapman worked for the American Museum of Natural History. He also

became active in the Audubon Society, campaigning for the conservation of birds. Was this later work perhaps fueled by his experience as a hunter and remorse for what he had done?

Chapman has gone down in history thanks to a very unusual census he conducted. While he was still working in finance, he took two afternoons off in 1886 to stroll down Fifth Avenue in Manhattan, looking for birds. And he found them. He tracked down forty species in all, which he meticulously recorded. They included laughing gulls, warblers, northern saw-whet owls, Virginia rails, and pine grosbeaks. He also recorded fifteen sightings of snow buntings. The birds, however, were not alive; they were not even stuffed. No, there were just bits and pieces of them on the heads of society ladies. The fact that more than three-quarters of the hats Chapman saw (542 out of 700 in just one afternoon) were trimmed with the feathers and sometimes even with the heads of birds gave a sense of how widespread the rage for feathers was at this time.

Chapman's appreciation for the power of numbers never left him. In 1900, he first raised the idea of a Christmas bird count to combat the then-popular Christmas "side hunt" for furred and feathered quarry, when Christmas parties divided up into teams or "sides" to see who could kill the most. At first, the Christmas Bird Count was just twenty-seven volunteers in twenty-five different locations in North America from Canada to California, but mostly in the highly populated areas of the northeast. The count followed a precisely prepared plan. On a single day within a three-week period, participants were to cover a specific area and precisely record all the birds they saw. The idea has since become so popular that every year, 7,000 amateur and professional bird watchers participate in a total of 2,200 locations all across the North American continent, in

---

Carolina parakeets by John James Audubon

Mexico, Colombia, Panama, in the West Indies, in Australia and its surrounding islands, and in the Pacific archipelagos of Melanesia, Polynesia, and Micronesia. The data collected during the count give valuable clues to population changes and are used by government agencies and ornithological organizations. Just recently, Adeline Murthy of the University of New Mexico used data gathered by Christmas Bird Count volunteers to show that eighteen species of birds can routinely be found in urban centers across North America—a clear indication that certain species of birds are gradually adapting to life in the city. The Christmas Bird Count, which has taken place every year since it was instituted, is the most comprehensive, ongoing wildlife census in the world.

Theodore Roosevelt (1858–1919)—a man who learned the craft of taxidermy at the age of eleven and later hunted waterfowl in the upper reaches of the Missouri—is one of the people we have to thank for putting an end to the somewhat ridiculous, and you might even say repulsive, fashion of putting birds on hats. While he was still governor of New York, he joined the Audubon Society's bird conservation movement and shut down the workshops that fashioned feathered hats. Despite this enlightened action, hunting still held him in its thrall. And so it was that even in the final years of his presidency (1901–09), he went on safari in British East Africa, and he and his companions returned with 5,013 mammals, 4,453 birds, and thousands of smaller animals that they had bagged.

THERE ARE ADVENTURERS who chase after birds with all the powers at their disposal in almost every region of the world. And the lengths to which they are prepared to go are an endless source of surprise. The Englishman Henry Seebohm (1832–95) was a Quaker who began collecting eggs and skins when he was still a schoolboy. He traveled, initially to Europe, with the same goal in mind. Wherever he went, he always shot as many birds as he could with his cane gun—an eminently practical combination of a shotgun built into a walking stick.

When Seebohm arrived at the Pechora river valley in the Ural Mountains in 1875, he was probably the first Englishman to visit the area in 250 years. When winter came, he and his friend and colleague John Harvie-Brown set off for Siberia after outfitting themselves in Vologda with fur coats, provisions, and a sled. If their horses balked, the two men drove them on by howling like wolves. (The expedition went through a total of 108 horses.) They soon encountered the Samoyeds, a nomadic people of Mongol descent. Always keen to profit from local knowledge, Seebohm visited a museum where stuffed birds were on display to learn their local

names. At first, the pair saw very few birds other than snow buntings. When they arrived in Ust Zylma, 300 miles (500 kilometers) from the mouth of the Pechora, they stopped to await the arrival of spring and the birds.

The thaw came at the beginning of May, and with it gulls, redstarts, and fish eagles. Seebohm soon spied a new species of warbler and other songbirds that he did not recognize. The explorers then traveled on to the mouth of the river by sailboat. In the delta with its "labyrinth of water and islands," the sun set so late that they could shoot birds to their hearts' content all night long. As the journey continued, they shot plovers and stole eggs from their nests. The birds had laid the eggs just recently, so they were perfect for a "superb" omelet for breakfast the following morning. Seebohm did not succeed in bagging a swan, but he managed to procure a skin by other means with a beak still attached. He was thrilled to ascertain that it was a rare Berwick's swan. Nearly one hundred years later, British ornithologist Peter M. Scott discovered that the yellow-and-black markings on the bills of these birds are unique to each individual.

Two years later, Seebohm traveled even farther east to the Yenisei, the fifth-longest river in the world. He undertook the almost 3,000-mile (5,000-kilometer) journey by sled in the company of a certain Captain Wiggins, who, he knew, had already traveled through the area. Once again, he wanted to talk with the indigenous people to find out what they knew about the birds. In this case, he was looking for the Khanty (formerly known as the Ostyaks), hunters who targeted birds and fur-bearing animals during the winter.

Seebohm spent much of the rest of his life analyzing the skins he brought back from his two Siberian expeditions. He established that many Siberian birds differ from members of the same species west of the Urals and subsequently decided, completely on his own, on a trinomial nomenclature that took these differences into account—a decision for which he was much criticized. He left seventeen thousand skins to the British Museum. One month before he died, he reportedly told his friends, "I can't sleep, because I have to think about the classification of birds." Legend has it that exactly at the moment his coffin was lowered into the ground, a thrush flew into a nearby tree and began to sing.

EMILIE SNETHLAGE (1868–1929) started observing birds early in her life and created a herbarium when she was still a child. Her father was a country parson who lost his wife early and had to raise his children on his own. In 1904, after studying natural sciences in Berlin, Jena, and Freiburg—studies made possible thanks to an inheritance she received—Snethlage became one of the first women in Germany to earn a doctorate. The following year, she moved to the Paraense Emílio Goeldi Museum in Belém, Brazil, and later became a naturalist at large in the service of the National Museum in Rio de Janeiro. In 1915, she was made an Honorary Lady Member of the British Ornithologists' Union, and a year later the German ornithological society granted her an honorary membership as well.

Apart from a few journeys to Europe, she concentrated on annual expeditions to tributaries of the Amazon, where she researched birds with a singular zeal. She was diminutive in stature but practically fearless and exceedingly resilient. She was unfazed when two young German scientists close to her were struck down by yellow fever, and when she experienced her first bout of malaria, she did her utmost to conceal the fact that she was ill. Her obituary in the *Journal für Ornithologie* (Journal of Ornithology) explained:

> *Strong willed as she was, she succeeded in hiding her fever from the Curuahé Indians who were escorting her from the River Iriri to the River Jamauchim. This was necessary because otherwise they would have left her alone in the wilderness thinking she was possessed by an evil spirit.*

Despite the original caption, this is actually a Lear's macaw by Edward Lear

When the middle finger of her right hand was almost torn off by piranhas, she had to amputate it herself because no one else was willing to do it. She was also good with a gun, and "in many regions she had the reputation of being a crack shot." In 1929, she and the German bird collector Emil Kaempfer climbed Pico da Bandeira in the Caparaó mountain range—which was believed at the time to be the highest mountain in the country. She lost her way on the descent and was forced to spend the night out in the open in freezing temperatures.

Snethlage thought of birds as her godchildren. Her husband reported that she often tracked them for days at a time before she killed them, and she only shot birds that she absolutely needed for her work.

> *She could sit for hours on a tree stump or crouched down on the ground. She kept annoying flies away from her face as best she could by smoking cigarettes, because the slightest movement of her hands would have frightened off the object of her attention.*

There are many dangers lurking in the tropics; Snethlage survived them all only to die of a heart attack. After her death, experts estimated that well over ten thousand birds and mammal skins in the collections of natural history museums all over the world had passed through her hands. Although Snethlage had set her heart on preparing a comprehensive catalog of the birds of Brazil, her *Catalogo das Aves Amazonicas* (Catalog of Amazonian Birds) was destined to remain unfinished.

ALSO ROAMING ABOUT in the Brazilian landscape was Helmut Sick (1910–91), who joined an expedition to Brazil in 1939. His name is most often associated with the story of the Lear's, or indigo, macaw, a large and incredibly noisy parrot painted by the legendary

British nonsense poet Edward Lear, who was very fond of parrots. (Lear wrote to a friend that "should any transmigration take place at my decease I am sure my soul would be very uncomfortable in anything but one of the Psittacidae.") For more than a century, the bird was one of the world's greatest ornithological puzzles. It was first described by Charles Lucien Bonaparte in 1856, after he came across a specimen in the National Museum of Natural History in Paris. In 1954, when Sick discovered that a Lear's macaw was apparently being kept as a house pet in the northeastern state of Pernambuco, he made it his personal quest to find the bird in the huge and impoverished Sertão region, which, up until then, had been nothing but a blank space on the ornithologists' maps. Although the region lies close to the equator, it offered little in the way of vegetation, suffered from droughts that lasted for months or even years, and, on top of all that, was exceedingly remote.

Putting on his detective's hat, Sick began to search for traces of the macaw, here and there uncovering clues, some more useful than others. It didn't help that the bird he sought was easily confused with other species of parrot, and specifically with the hyacinth macaw, which is the same blue as the indigo but considerably larger. As time went on, he undertook two more expeditions to check out all the places where the bird had been spotted. Things were not looking good for the last research expedition in the summer of 1978–79. Sick developed a hernia, and because he could not get a truss while the expedition was underway, it was only with the greatest of efforts that he could keep it under control. Added to that, in the early days of travel, he was suffering from a bout of malaria. He later wrote with restrained humor, "I was on the trail of the rarest bird in the world with my insides hanging out."

At first the expedition drew a blank. Then, at the end of December, a hunter offered Sick blue feathers that obviously came from the bird he was looking for—physical proof that the bird still existed in the wild. The hunter said he had killed it just a few weeks earlier for its meat. After an extensive search, on the last day of the year, the members of the expedition finally met with success when they spotted about twenty birds in flight. About ten days later, Sick caught sight of a pair of Lear's macaws through his spotting scope as they flew to their roosting site in a canyon, where "they were surrounded by a dense cloud of insects and sometimes scratched themselves on the head."

As soon as Sick killed one of the birds and divulged where he had found them, he would put himself in an awkward position, for his mission was to protect the birds that remained. In the end, he proudly announced:

> *I have succeeded in solving the greatest puzzle in the ornithology of South America (not only in Brazil)—the discovery of the origin of the Lear's Macaw, a magnificent large blue macaw [29 inches/74 centimeters from head to tail]... which until now was only known from specimens in captivity. I had searched in vain twice before. This time I came to exactly the right place, the Raso da Catarina in the state of Bahia, the last remaining place, according to my calculations, where these birds could be hiding.*

We will leave it to the experts to decide if he discovered the bird or merely rediscovered it. In any event, the puzzle was solved and Sick achieved his goal. The bird, which mainly feeds on the small nuts from the scarce licurí palm, is currently listed as endangered.

BERTRAM "BILL" E. SMYTHIES (1912–99) did not need to emigrate to get to know exotic landscapes, because he came into the world in Uttar Pradesh, India, the son of an Indian Forest Service employee. His trips to the mountains began when he was still a baby, and he traced his love of birds back to these early experiences: "[I] started

hill trekking at the age of six months, camping in tents in the hills of Kumaon... brought up within sight of Nanda Devi and Trisul—who could fail to have a love of mountains and natural history?"

After studying botany and forestry at Oxford, England, in 1934, he entered the forest service in Burma (now Myanmar) and had the opportunity to explore the country's remote mountain regions. Shortly thereafter, he had an idea for a book about the birds of Burma. However, gathering material came with many complications.

> *Bearing in mind the fact that there is no museum in Burma whence skins can be borrowed, the difficulty of assembling models for each of the 290 birds illustrated in this book can be appreciated; some birds were painted from live examples in the Rangoon Zoo, chiefly waders and game birds; a few were copied from paintings in other books; but the majority had to be collected in the fields and the forests and the marshes, by those responsible for the book, in their spare time.*

The search for a few of the birds lasted a year or more. Some were too tasty for their own good, and birds, once bagged, had to be drawn quickly in Burma's tropical heat.

> *There was the great barbet, not a rare bird, but a shy one, which we chased unavailingly up and down the slopes of Nattaung for a week and more without success....[t]he masked finfoot, a rarity that we hardly hoped to find except by dispatching a special mission to its known haunts in the flooded jungles of the Myitmaka drainage, but which gaily swam into Smith's ken, much to his astonishment, in a totally unexpected place on a back-water of the Pegu river; and there was the sad story of the argus pheasant, pride of the Rangoon Zoo, which died mysteriously in its cage immediately after its portrait had been painted and was forthwith skinned and stuffed by the artist (roast argus, it was hinted, was delicious); and the three vultures, freshly skinned and exuding a foul and sticky odour, are to this day a vivid and unhappy memory for the artist's wife, who had to endure them in the house till their portraits had been finished.*

And as if that were not enough, Smythies had to send to England for some skins he needed to fill gaps in his collection. *Birds of Burma,* however, became a classic work on the avian world of

Southeast Asia. At first, the book, which was printed in Rangoon, was bought mostly by Europeans living in Burma. During World War II, Smythies had to move to the north of the country. His father was by then a forester for the maharaja of Nepal, and Smythies got permission to visit him. There, up at the Ganja La Pass, he was able to study birds that lived at high elevations in the Himalayas. When the Japanese occupied Burma between 1942 and 1945, they assumed—erroneously—that his book contained the key to a secret code because they found a copy in all the best military households. The Japanese confiscated all the copies they could lay their hands on, and these were later destroyed in an American bombing raid on Japan. In a daring move, Smythies managed to lay his hands on the copper plates from which the engravings of the birds had been printed and spirited them out of the country and to safety in India.

Smythies was able to continue his work in Burma until the country gained its independence in 1948, primarily because the Japanese never made it to the north. After that, he spent fifteen years in Sarawak on the island of Borneo—which at that time was still under British military rule—before moving to Europe. His bird book was reprinted twice, and Smythies died while working on the fourth edition.

NOT EVERYONE WHO worked under similarly challenging conditions managed to safeguard their work. Allan Octavian Hume (1829–1912) was a Scot who worked for the Indian Civil Service for decades. He is credited with a number of educational reforms, was involved at the highest levels with the establishment of the Indian National Congress, and knew the Indian subcontinent better than most of his contemporaries. While he was director general for agriculture, he built up a network of more than fifty bird collectors who provided him with birds from every region in India and Burma, which allowed him to compile the most comprehensive collection of Asiatic birds of his time. The collection, together with a specialist reference library, was housed at Rothney Castle in Simla, in the far north of the country. He employed a gardener at the castle and was known for his hospitality. Along with his other activities, he was president of the local theosophical society, a popular organization at the time that strove to serve humanity by respecting the unity of life.

In 1872, Hume established the periodical *Stray Feathers—A Journal of Ornithology for India and Its Dependencies,* published books (including *Game Birds of India, Burma and Ceylon*), and undertook numerous expeditions. In Burma he was presented with feathers from a bird as-yet-unknown to science and after a further search was undertaken, living examples of the species were also delivered. It turned out to be a new species of pheasant and was named in his honor: *Syrmaticus humiae.*

Hume's next project was to compile a comprehensive record of the birds of India. In the winter of 1884, he left his castle in the mountains to spend the winter months in the milder climate of the plains. On his return in the spring, he discovered to his horror that his manuscript, including additional documents and correspondence, had been sold as scrap paper at the bazaar. With that, not only was twenty-five years of work consigned to oblivion, but he also lost all enthusiasm for ornithology. He decided to shut down his collection and sell it to the Natural History Museum in London. Given the transportation options at the time, this was a logistical nightmare. However, he managed to pull it off, and everything arrived safe and sound. He left India and returned to England, where he founded a botanical institute. Despite turning his back on birds, Hume is considered to be not just the father but indeed the pope of Indian ornithology. Today there is nothing to remember him in Simla but ruins—where the avian inhabitants of the area are more than happy to spend their time.

THE DUTCH BEHAVIORAL biologist and Nobel Prize winner Nikolaas Tinbergen believed that excessive bird watching is an expression of the "male hunting instincts," and the British psychologist and autism researcher Simon Baron-Cohen describes it as the "male tendency for systemizing," but, as we have already seen in this chapter, not all who are driven to hunt down birds—either literally or metaphorically—are male. Beryl Patricia Hall (1917–2010) proved she was made of stern stuff back when she worked as an ambulance driver for the British army in the Egyptian desert. Later, she worked at the Natural History Museum in London for decades, and was known there for participating in a variety of birding expeditions. Her travels took her to South Africa, southwestern Africa, and Central Australia. In 1957, she participated in the first Pan-African Ornithological Congress, which was held in Livingstone, in what was then Northern Rhodesia (now Zambia), near the world-famous Victoria Falls. Part of the reason for her attendance was so that after the congress she could make a side trip to Angola to track down one of the rarest birds in Africa: the Angola cave chat *(Xenocopsychus ansorgei)*. She was successful in her mission. When bird conservationists voiced qualms about the carnage wrought on that trip, she countered by commenting that four collectors killing fewer than two hundred birds in four days did no more damage to the population than would be inflicted by a cat over the course of a year.

On one occasion, Hall described the special challenges connected to the act of stuffing birds:

> *Oddly it is not the actual skinning of the birds that causes most difficulty, though when making a specimen for scientific use one has to take great care not to either split the skin more than necessary or to let blood or juices from the stomach stain the feathers: the real difficulty is in making up the skin to life size so that all feathers lie correctly; a few wrinkles or stretches in the skin or a stitch pulled too tight can make the final result look like a feather duster.*

ELIZABETH VLADIMIROVNA KOZLOVA (1892–1975) was another of those ornithologists (like Henry Seebohm before her) who were not put off by a little bad weather. In 1923, she joined her husband, Petr Kozlov, on an expedition to Mongolia on behalf of the Russian Imperial Geographical Society as an ornithologist. This was to be more than just a fleeting visit. All told, she spent three years in Transbaikal and in the Kentei and Changai Mountains. There she heard nutcrackers, cuckoos, black woodpeckers, pine grosbeaks, crossbills, snipe, and many other birds that were little known at the time. She wrote that the mating calls of the capercaillie reminded her of the clapping sound of castanets. She tracked the numerous species that overwintered in the valleys across the mostly snow-free, south-facing slopes and continued tracking them even when she encountered deep snow. In late summer, she crossed the salt lakes and steppes of the northern Gobi Desert to winter in the southern foothills of the Changai Mountains so she would be ready to observe birds from the shores of Ozero Orok-nur Lake when they returned the following spring. Together with her colleagues, she collected 1,700 birds from 306 species and subspecies, which were incorporated into the inventory of the Zoological Institute of the Russian Academy of Sciences in Leningrad. Kozlova returned to Mongolia for another two winters—1929 and 1930. After that, she turned her attention to the Caspian Sea and then, during World War II, to Tajikistan. Later, she worked at her desk in Leningrad and wrote books about the birds of the Soviet Union and Mongolia.

EVEN IN THE latter part of the twentieth century, there were people who spent a good deal of time as passionate hunters before they embraced conservation. Boonsong Lekagul (1907–92), a Thai medical doctor, made a name for himself in the 1930s and 1940s as an enthusiastic big game hunter until he realized after World War II that all manner of human factors were contributing to the disappearance of wildlife. He once compared his sudden change of heart with the opening of a bud into a "wonderful, beautiful flower," and he vowed to do everything in his power to stem the tide of destruction. Despite his vow, he shot about ten thousand birds over the next ten years for his museum; however—and you could see this as a justification or not, as you wish—the activity was no longer a sport for him but a question of science.

He concentrated his initial conservation efforts on the openbill stork, which flew in from India to breed and had just one remaining colony in Thailand. The colony was on the grounds of a ramshackle Buddhist monastery on the banks of the Chao Phraya River in Wat Pai Lom, north of Bangkok. When he publicized the birds' situation, he successfully raised funds for a new building and a small bird sanctuary. The area exists to this day, and at certain times of the year, you can also find spot-billed pelicans, black-capped kingfishers, and black-headed ibis there. He also developed a program to train guides to lead field trips, not only to spot birds but also to observe butterflies and small mammals. Boonsong, who became known across Southeast Asia as Mr. Conservation, published his *Bird Guide of Thailand* in 1968 and *A Guide to the Birds of Thailand* in 1991.

{ 12 }

Flight Trackers

IT HAS BEEN said of Danish schoolteacher Hans Christian Cornelius Mortensen (1856–1921) that this gigantic man possessed enormous physical strength, could run for hours at a time, and could scale any tree he encountered. One observer described him as being "like a tiger." He was openly opposed to coffee, tobacco, and alcohol, and he always wore a dark suit with large pockets that looked rather like a uniform. Mortensen was convinced that yellow paper was gentler on the eyes than white paper, and therefore always wore yellow-tinted eye protection. His single-mindedness and drive helped him to pursue what was in his day a revolutionary new extracurricular activity. A diverse selection of experts had agonized over such questions as whether the migratory routes of birds can be attributed to instinct, whether birds have an innate sense of direction, and why they follow specific features in the landscape. Mortensen was interested in a more practical question: How could one reliably mark birds without interfering with their ability to fly? In an 1849 paper in the ornithological journal *Rhea,* he discovered evidence that half a century before, in the course of a multiyear attempt to tame wild geese and ducks, a Dutchman named Baron van der Heyden had placed a brass ring around the neck of a goose that was shot thirty years later near Danzig. He seized upon the idea of putting bands on birds, which led many people to think he was mad (or possibly reinforced existing thoughts of his madness).

On June 6, 1890, Mortensen furnished two young starlings with thin tin bands with "Viborg 1890" inscribed on both the inside and outside, but he soon realized that tin was too heavy. In 1899, he switched to aluminum, and before the year was out, he had outfitted 162 starlings with his new bands. He had thought his plan through down to the last detail. Because aluminum is rough when cut, he asked his students to carry the bands around in small bags filled with sand until the edges were polished smooth. Since he had petitioned many of his friends to mention his experiment in the professional literature, he soon received news that banded birds had been shot in both the Netherlands and Norway. His appearance at the International Ornithological Congress in Paris in 1900 helped make the procedure he had devised more widely known.

IT IS ONE thing to discover the aerial routes of birds and their connection to seasons, fluctuations in the weather, and changes in air pressure; it is quite another to tease out the reasons underlying these movements. Many people have been involved in investigating the mystery of migration, which has still not been completely explained, and they often devoted large parts of their lives to answering this question, sometimes proposing ambitious and downright fanciful theories.

The ornithologist and artist Heinrich Gätke (1814–97) came to Heligoland as an artist and—fascinated by bird migration—stayed on for sixty years. He worked as a government secretary for the British administration there. Gätke believed, somewhat unusually, that the spring migration was always led by the most "beautifully colored" mature males. They "spread the word," and the mature females appeared a week or two later. The fall migration (in all species, no less) was, he believed, led by the younger birds.

In the 1920s, Alex Stimmelmayr and his brother Anton shipped bluethroats from Potsdam to Landshut and Munich, and then shipped redstarts in the opposite direction. Some of the birds could be found two weeks later at the locations where they had been caught. Stimmelmayr was soon applying himself to what he called the "secret of the sun in bird migration," and a short time later he arrived at what he cryptically referred to as the "cosmic problem" in bird migration. When the National Socialists came to power in Germany, he found that people were no longer interested in his conjectures on what he described in 1942 as "the great mystery of space and time in the natural cycles of life." After World War II, he wrote about the apparent effects of the sun's and Earth's energy fields on migration. This time he was onto something, as we now know that some birds—carrier pigeons, for example—use Earth's magnetic fields to orient themselves on long journeys.

Bird research also got a boost at this time from the ever-increasing number of people who went up into the air and were privileged to observe birds from small planes, as well as from connections forged between ornithology and earth sciences (such as the ones that led to research into how pigeons use Earth's magnetic fields). And for decades, tiny, feather-light transmitters with satellite connections have offered new opportunities for collecting data on the enormous distances covered by migrating birds and the routes they take, including details about the distances they cover in a day and the speed at which they fly.

AIR TRAVEL REVOLUTIONIZED migration research. In Carroll Ballard's 1996 movie *Fly Away Home*, Canada geese follow an ultralight aircraft. The movie begins with the story of Amy, a lonely little girl who takes an abandoned clutch of sixteen goslings under her wing that then become imprinted on her. Because the geese cannot make their way to their wintering grounds without outside help, Amy's father comes up with the idea of leading them from Ontario to North Carolina with a small plane. After many complications and minor upsets, the plan succeeds. The movie was based on the story of a Canadian inventor named Walter Lishman, who accompanied Canada geese with his plane in 1993. Of the sixteen geese in the group, thirteen managed to return without help. Lishman is considered to be a pioneer in the field of learned flight behavior. Since then, Operation Migration has led several attempts to reintroduce whooping cranes—one of the rarest species of birds in the world—to the eastern United States.

SCOTT WEIDENSAUL INTRODUCED a global dimension to bird migration in his book *Living on the Wind*. According to estimates, no fewer than five billion birds take to the air on annual migrations. Weidensaul compared the patterns of bird migration to "great weather systems, which roar out from the poles but fizzle at the equator." He argued that the act of migration was "perhaps the most compelling drama in all of natural history." Trying to dispel misconceptions about migration, Weidensaul underscored that migration is not "the simple, north-to-south-and-back-again affair" that most of us assume, and in his ongoing research, he tries to measure the threats to migratory birds from habitat loss and environmental degradation as and when they arise.

I had the opportunity to ask Weidensaul how it all began for him. This is what he told me:

In a nutshell, I got started with birds (and with nature in general) at such an early age that I can't recall a time when I wasn't [involved],

although my fascination with migration had a very clear begin-ning. One day, when I was twelve, my parents took me to Hawk Mountain Sanctuary in eastern Pennsylvania—not far from our home—a famous migratory choke point for tens of thousands of rap-tors. Watching hawks, falcons, and the occasional eagle drift down the ridge in a long, majestic parade hooked me for life on three things: birds of prey, the Appalachian mountain system along which they were traveling, and the phenomenon of migration. (And Hawk Moun-tain, which became the world's first refuge for birds of prey when it was founded in 1934, remains central to me as well; I currently serve on its board of directors.) It's been a long, twisting road since then.

Weidensaul is actively involved in a number of projects. He and colleagues formed Project SNOWstorm, which makes use of the lat-est tracking technology to study snowy owls. He is founder of the Critical Connections project, which tracks the migration of birds that breed in Denali National Park in Alaska. And he is also part of a continent-wide effort to understand rapid evolutionary changes in several species of western hummingbirds that are altering their tra-ditional migratory routes and their wintering ranges in eastern and southeastern North America.

LET US CONCLUDE this chapter with the heartwarming (or possi-bly heartbreaking, depending on your point of view) story of two devoted storks. One stork, which goes by the name of Klepetan, has been observed flying to the same rooftop in the village of Slavon-ski Brod in East Croatia every year for the past fourteen years (at time of writing). He travels all the way from Africa, a journey of 5,000 miles (8,000 kilometers), where he spends the winters alone, to be reunited with his disabled partner, Malena, who was shot by a hunter in 1993 and has since been unable to migrate. Each winter, villager Stepan Vokic keeps Malena in his house. He lets her out so that she can go up to the roof each spring, where she waits for her partner. The stork couple still raise a brood of chicks each summer. People are so fascinated by the lives of these two birds that there is a live feed broadcast in the main square in the capital, Zagreb.

{ 13 }

The Lure of the Egg

THE SCIENCE OF eggs is called "oology" (from the Greek "oion") and not, as one might have guessed, "ovology." Is interest in the outer covering of an egg an expression of the joy the observer feels as they anticipate the new life forming unseen inside? That is doubtful, because the act of collecting blown eggshells and storing them in boxes, drawers, and cupboards—taking them out from time to time to dust them off—pretty much shoots that theory down. Is there any connection at all between marveling at the object and appreciating the bird? It hardly seems possible that the urge to collect eggs and delight in bird watching could coexist in the mind of one person. Perhaps it is only the egg in all its flawless perfection that fascinates, and what the observer experiences is an appreciation for the object in and of itself?

Until the latter half of the nineteenth century, egg collecting was a particularly popular pastime among bird lovers. Even though collecting eggs came with its own set of challenges, the eggs, unlike bird skins, did not need any special treatment to make them last so they could be stored and displayed. All collectors needed to do was blow them out. However, it has to be said that it is often difficult to identify individual eggs in a collection, because although all kinds of claims can be made about an egg, it is impossible to prove the exact species an individual egg belongs to or exactly where it was collected. You have no choice but to rely on information provided by the collector. To complicate matters, disreputable collectors sometimes painted their eggs to match those of rarer species so they could charge unsuspecting buyers a higher price.

OOLOGY WAS OFTEN connected to far-fetched theories that make no sense to us today. For example, Jean Guillaume Rey (1838–1909), an introverted individual who was born into a French emigrant family in Berlin and who practiced chemistry at home, owned a large collection of birds' eggs and was particularly interested in the brood parasitism of cuckoos. He tried to draw connections between the patterns on birds' eggs and how birds were classified.

Ornithological journals were first published in the nineteenth century, and eggs were always a hot topic in them. There were reports of misshapen eggs—eggs with flat sides or sharply pointed ends, or long, thin eggs with grooves along their sides. There were also "eggs within eggs," which came in different shapes—usually, an egg the size of a walnut and without a yolk was found within a larger egg. From the way they wrote about them, you would be forgiven for thinking that collectors believed in the magical powers of eggs, although they stopped short of crediting them with the supernatural properties sometimes conferred upon them by non-Western cultures.

THERE WERE SOME outstanding collectors. As co-owner of a business trading in natural history specimens, Franz Kricheldorff (1853–1924) traveled to China and Tibet on collecting expeditions on behalf of such patrons as Lord Walter Rothschild. Apart from

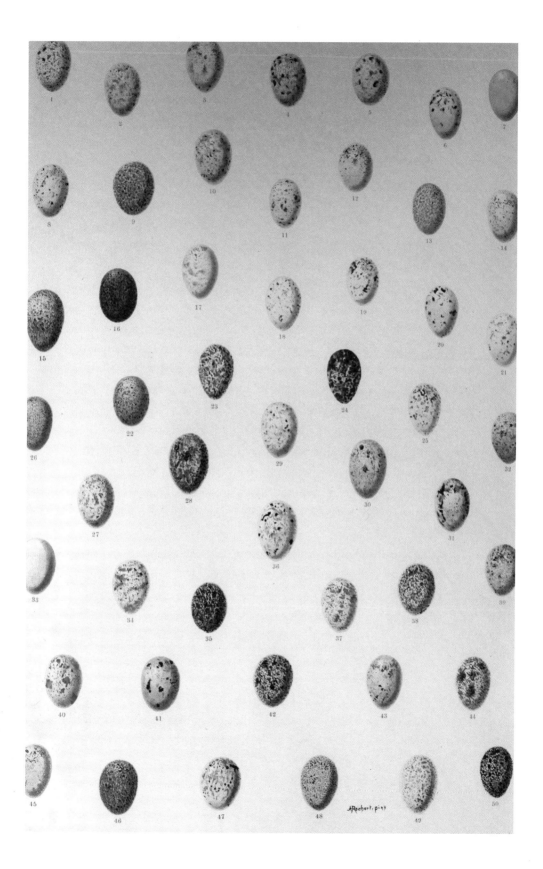

his commercial activities, he also maintained a comprehensive and important egg collection, which he had built up over decades. One connoisseur once called it "a testament to German industry and aptitude." The collection included 310 cuckoo eggs, most of which were collected from warbler nests.

Some egg collectors were so obsessive that not just any egg would do. In his book *The Most Perfect Thing*, biologist Tim Birkhead tells the tale of George Lupton, a wealthy lawyer from Yorkshire, England, in the 1930s who commissioned those who plundered nests on the limestone cliffs of Bempton to procure for him the same beautiful brown eggs with unique markings from the same female guillemot (murre) every year—for two decades. His focus on this unfortunate bird meant that for all of her breeding life she "never once succeeded in hatching an egg or rearing a chick."

When he was six, Max Schönwetter (1874–1961), who later became a surveyor, found the remains of a partridge egg with blood vessels still sticking to it, which is said to have provoked in him an unquenchable desire to study birds' eggs. Over the course of sixty years, and with the help of people who traveled, he amassed a private collection that included the eggs of almost four thousand species of birds. The smallest egg—from a bee hummingbird— was the size of a pea. It was one-fifth of an inch (5 millimeters) long and weighed in at an infinitesimal fraction of an ounce (one-quarter of a gram). Schönwetter brought that delicate object, as well as a 3½-pound (1.6-kilogram) ostrich egg and all the other eggs in his collection, unscathed through two world wars. According to ornithological historian Ludwig Gebhardt:

> *In his old age the confirmed bachelor could claim to have examined more eggs than any other person alive or dead, and no other method of comparing eggs was more thoroughly thought through or more detailed in its methods than the one he had devised.*

His lifelong study of the morphology of eggshells, which he pursued with dogged determination while surmounting repeated troubles, disappointments, and difficulties, culminated in 1952 with the publication of his life's work, *Handbuch der Oologie* (Handbook of Oology).

Another particularly noteworthy collector was Alexis Romanoff (1892–1980), a Russian who immigrated to the United States in 1921. Shortly after he arrived, he began to devote his life to eggs. While he was studying for his doctorate at Cornell University, he decided to publish the world's most authoritative book on the biology of the egg. He worked on it for twenty long years along with his wife, Anastasia—day in, day out, including evenings and weekends, distracted by neither children nor travel. *The Avian Egg*, almost 1,000 pages long with 435 illustrations, appeared in 1949 and was a huge success with experts in the field.

THE FIRST BIRD lovers to express concern about and argue against the damaging and unnecessary practice of egg collecting began clamoring to be heard in the middle of the nineteenth century. Toward the end of the century, they were increasingly attracting the attention of bird conservationists and soon after that, the law makers. For the American nature writer John Burroughs (1837–1921), egg and skin collectors were "men who plunder nests and murder their owners." At the annual meeting of the Royal Society for the Protection of Birds in 1922, a warning was finally given about the "distinct menace" posed by the egg collectors, whereupon Lord Walter Rothschild, who felt he had been slighted, split off from the Royal Society and helped found the British Oological Association. Dedicated to egg collecting, it was later renamed the Jourdain Society after one of its founding partners. Meetings of the association were targeted by police in the 1990s—it is a mystery how they managed to meet for so long—and more than half the members were

fined for illegal possession of eggs. Like members of a terrorist organization, members hid their identities when they were interviewed. The ban on collecting eggs of protected species of birds seems to have merely increased the appeal of doing exactly that.

THE MOST COMPREHENSIVE collection of birds' eggs in the world can be found at the Natural History Museum at Tring in England (which came under the direction of the Natural History Museum in London in the late 1930s). It comprises approximately two million specimens. The eggs are stored in the basement in locked cabinets. The collection garnered attention in the 1960s when Derek Ratcliffe (1929–2005) was researching why peregrine falcons were not breeding successfully. When he compared their eggshells with older ones from the museum, he noticed how thin they had become, a defect that was linked to pesticide use. Later, DDT was banned throughout Europe.

THE NAMES OF some egg collectors are inextricably linked with criminal activity. Take, for example, Londoner Matthew Gonshaw, who had already served three prison sentences when he was convicted in 2004 for having collected 600 eggs, 104 of which he had hidden in a secret compartment in his bed frame. Typically, he wore camouflage when he went egg hunting and carried not only topographical maps, a climbing rope, and a survival manual like those used by the military, but also a whole battery of syringes he used to remove the contents of the eggs on the spot.

Then there is the remarkable case of Mervyn Shorthouse, who was convicted in 1979 of having, over the course of three years—during which he visited the Tring museum at least once a week—made away with an estimated ten thousand eggs. As a regular visitor, he had gained the trust of the staff and aroused no suspicion, because he posed as a wheelchair-bound invalid. The museum could perhaps have recovered from the loss of the eggs; however, because Shorthouse wanted to cover up the theft, he mixed up all the labels, thus considerably reducing the value of the most comprehensive historical collection in the world. Shorthouse is the reason the collection is carefully locked away today.

Compulsive egg collecting is not confined to Great Britain. For example, in the recent past, police in Finland confiscated ten thousand eggs from the house of a man who was suspected of being a member of a network of Scandinavian egg collectors, some of whom were trading in the eggs of protected species.

One particularly special egg that has not yet fallen into the clutches of the egg mafia is the only one that remains from Charles Darwin's legendary journey on HMS *Beagle*. It was discovered by chance in 2009 in the zoological museum at Cambridge University in England, when a volunteer was cataloguing the collection—at the time she found the egg she was ten years into her task. The egg is probably from a spotted nothura from Uruguay. The dark-colored specimen is cracked and bears the name C. Darwin. The shell cracked when Darwin tried to put the egg into a box that was just a little too small for it. "To have discovered a *Beagle* specimen in the 200th year of Darwin's birth is special enough, but to have evidence that Darwin himself broke it is a wonderful twist," collections manager Mathew Lowe reported.

MODERN OOLOGISTS GO beyond eggs as objects and research them to discover what they might tell us about the birds themselves and their behavior. Birkhead reports in his book on the ways that guillemot (murre) eggs are designed to resist contamination by guano in the messy environs of their colonies: their surfaces are covered with "a mass of pointy peaks" to keep the guano off and they are laid narrow end first—which is unusual, but ensures that the wider end that encloses the chick's head and air cell remains relatively feces-free. Guillemot eggs are also longer than most birds' eggs, helping to keep them grounded on the rocky ledges where guillemots make their nests. British researchers Emma J.A. Cunningham and Andrew F. Russell have found that female mallards invest in larger eggs when they mate with more attractive males. Beautiful as they are, there really is more to eggs than meets the eye.

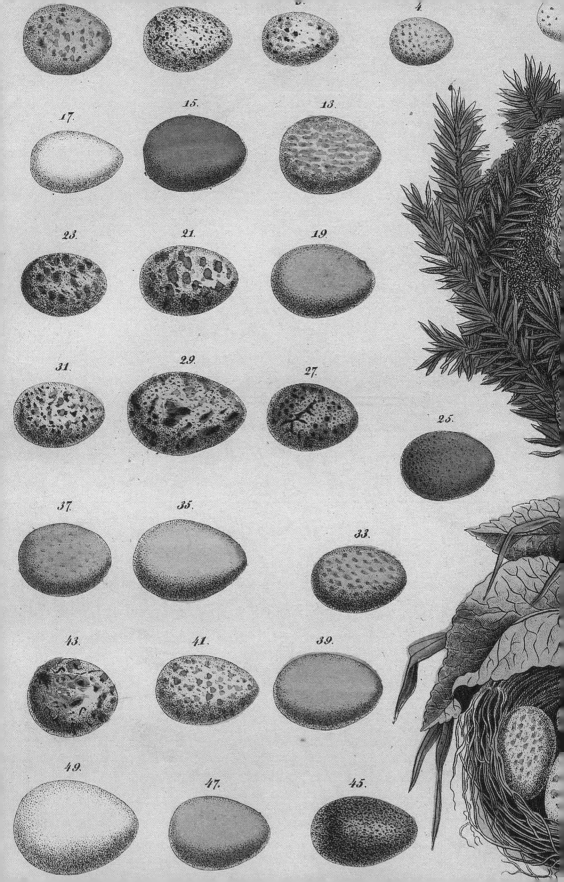

{ 14 }

Focus on Feathers

ROXIE C. LAYBOURNE (1912–2003) was a special kind of specialist. She worked at the Smithsonian National Museum for
Natural History for more than half a century, where she developed procedures to help airplane manufacturers reduce the risk of
midair collisions with birds. Based on her investigations of feathers
and the remains of bones, she identified which species of birds were
involved in airplane accidents. Starlings are one species that pose
a safety risk, thanks to their habit of massing in large numbers in
areas around airports. In 1960, six minutes after take-off, a flock of
around ten thousand of them flew into the flight path of a Lockheed
Elektra, a propeller-driven passenger plane, after it took off from
Logan International Airport, in Boston, Massachusetts. It crashed
and broke up in a nearby bay. Sixty-two of the seventy-two passengers lost their lives. To this day, it is the most dramatic bird-related
aviation incident in history. Laybourne—who in the course of her
career acquired nicknames such as "the feather detective" and "the
Miss Marple of Eiderdown"—was assigned the case and was able to
clearly identify the culprits.

Today we know that gulls are responsible for almost one-third of such incidents, with others being caused by geese, waterfowl, pigeons, blackbirds, and birds of prey, to name a few of the most frequent offenders. As soon as the species of bird has been identified, preventative measures are taken in the area around the airport in question to keep the birds away. At Seattle-Tacoma (Sea-Tac) airport, south of Seattle, hawks can be a problem. A local organization, the Falcon Research Group, has a hawk relocation program. They collect the hawks, tag them, and release them farther north in hawk heaven, otherwise known as the Skagit Valley. To date, no hawks have been known to return to the airport. A local shuttle bus company transports the birds from the airport to the valley free of charge. So, if you arrive in Sea-Tac one day and take the shuttle north, don't be surprised if you find yourself sharing a ride with a hawk.

Although most airplanes today are designed to withstand bird collisions better, there is still a risk, and every couple of years there are accidents that cost human lives. In 2009 in Louisiana, a falcon flew into a helicopter windshield, and eight of the nine passengers lost their lives in the ensuing crash. In the same year, a passenger plane with 155 people on board had to make an emergency landing in the Hudson River in New York. Dubbed "Miracle on the Hudson" because Captain Chesley "Sully" Sullenberger managed to land the Airbus A320 with no loss of life, an investigation of the bird remains revealed that Canada geese had knocked out both of the plane's engines. In 2016, the story of this accident was made into the movie *Sully*, starring Tom Hanks.

Laybourne was consulted for her expertise in other cases, as well. In at least two murder investigations, her specialized knowledge

---

Roxie Laybourne at work

helped solve the crimes. In a job for the FBI, she identified the feathers in a coat that washed up on the Pacific coast. Her investigation revealed that the feathers were from a Chinese duck and were an exact match for feathers found in the delivery van of a man who turned out to have murdered his wife in Alaska and thrown her body into the sea. The woman's body was never found. In another case, a woman was convicted of shooting her husband while he was asleep. In order to muffle the sound of the shot, she had wrapped the gun in a feather pillow. Laybourne found microscopic traces of feathers in the victim's brain that were a positive match for the feathers in the perforated pillow.

Today, the appropriately named ornithologist Carla Dove continues Laybourne's work. This is what she wrote to me about her former colleague:

Roxie loved birds and watching birds. In fact, she watched birds up until her death in 2003. She would sit in her log cabin out in Manassas and look out the big picture window at the feeder even when she was no longer driving in to work. She did not have pet birds. She did not want anything "alive" in the house to take care of. She also helped many Boy Scouts, young students, and colleagues learn about birds and how to be a real birdwatcher. Roxie's passion was birds and it didn't matter if she was at work or at home or on the road, she always had her binoculars and always wanted to learn more about birds.

IT WAS THE vultures he met while on a research expedition to Kenya that led the American biologist Thor Hanson to explore the world of feathers. And he made several discoveries. Vultures' feathers repel bacteria—which is important as the birds have such a messy job to do—and absorb the heat of the African sun—which helps the birds keep warm when they cruise high in the sky searching for their next meal. Hanson was fascinated by the way feathers influence every aspect of the lives of birds. They can camouflage birds or make them stand out; they can absorb water or repel it. Nothing is as unique to birds as feathers. According to Hanson, for whom feathers are a passion, they are the lightest and most efficient insulating material ever.

Hanson decided that to understand feathers, he needed to take a good close look at them. After toying with the idea of dispatching one of his chickens, "a surly old Wyandotte who'd never been much of a layer," he came across a winter wren in his freezer, "nestled between the halibut and old soup," a roadkill he had tucked away for future investigation and then forgotten about. He decided to pluck the wren, but the only reference he had on hand that might give him guidance was that kitchen staple *The Joy of Cooking*. Irma S. Rombauer, the author, "didn't offer any recipes specific to wrens," but she did have a section on wild game, and she recommended plucking them cold. Luckily, the wren had not yet thawed out completely, and Hanson set to armed with a pair of tweezers and some needle-nosed pliers. He was enthralled by the feathers he ended up with, describing the down feathers from the belly as being "so soft their touch was like the faintest brush of air, less a sensation than an anticipation." Hanson is so devoted to feathers that he also counts them—from the 1,000 feathers of a ruby-throated hummingbird to the 25,000 of a tundra swan. If you were to take all the feathers in the world and lay them end to end, Hanson has calculated, they would reach not only to the sun, but way beyond. After reading Hanson, you might be tempted to think that feathers are the secret motor that drives the world.

{ 15 }

Mad for Bird Watching

THE ESTIMATED NUMBER of species of birds in the world has fluctuated significantly over the centuries. After Aristotle took a good look around where he lived in the Mediterranean and came up with 140 species, the number rose exponentially in the eighteenth and nineteenth centuries until, at the beginning of the twentieth century, it had escalated to almost 19,000—a number that was then reduced to about 8,600 starting in the early 1940s. For a long time, a bird could be described as "new," because no one had a bird's eye view of the situation. How could anyone have known that a longclaw found in the Russian Arctic in 1875 had already been shot and described in southwestern China a few years before? Birds that are difficult to differentiate from similar species, such as redpolls and crossbills, could have ten or more different names. In *A History of Birds of Europe 1871*, Henry Dresser lists sixty-four different noteworthy names for the crested lark, taking up a full two pages of the book. Today, based on further discoveries and DNA analysis, the number of species stands at 10,500, assigned to just

200 different families, all of them fascinating in their own unique ways, and many of them flying, hopping, and, maybe, just perching, waiting to be watched by an interested person equipped with a pair of binoculars or, perhaps, just with the naked eye.

There are examples of people carefully observing bird behavior before watching birds became a popular pastime in the twentieth century. The English country doctor and naturalist Edward Jenner (1749–1823) comes to mind. He not only made a huge contribution to humanity by developing the smallpox vaccine (hence his nickname "father of immunology"), but—following in Aristotle's footsteps—also spent fifteen years observing the behavior of cuckoos. He discovered that a young cuckoo pushes each of its "step-siblings" out of the nest individually, until it is the only one remaining to be fed. We have Jenner to thank for brood parasitism being such a well-known fact today—although it possible, of course, that someone else would have come across it sooner or later. His observations, which were later confirmed using photography, garnered him his nomination as a Fellow of the Royal Society in 1789.

THE INVENTOR OF the term "bird watching," used by millions of people around the world to describe this pastime today, was British ornithologist and author Edmund Selous (1857–1934). *Bird Watching* was the title of a handbook he published in 1901, but the activity he described was very different from what we understand as bird watching today. In those days, the only fresh air bird watchers got was when they were on the trail of eggs or skins. The rest of their time was spent admiring the collections they had stashed in cupboards and drawers. The science of ornithology was no different. When Selous entered the field, the study of dead birds gathering dust in museum display cabinets was favored over the study of live birds going about their business in the outdoors. When live birds were considered suitable subjects for study, it was under conditions

controlled by scientists in their laboratories and not in the wild where the birds could come and go as they pleased. These ivory-tower experts considered themselves to be the "zoologists of the future," but Selous was a very different kind of researcher, and his relationship with his peers was never a comfortable one.

Like many other ornithologists of his day, he had started out with a gun in his hand, but the more he watched birds, the less he wanted to kill them.

For myself, I must confess that I once belonged to this great, poor army of killers, though happily, a bad shot... But now that I have watched birds closely, the killing of them seems to me as something monstrous and horrible.

For Selous, precise observation of animals behaving naturally was his holy grail. His first scientific article, about a pair of nesting

Margaret Morse Nice

nightjars that he had observed at close quarters using a nearby elderberry bush as cover, appeared in 1899. In his field studies in the following three decades, he concentrated, above all, on bird behavior, including mate selection and flock dynamics.

Selous made a point of not relying on the work of others before him, and he did not recognize anything as a fact until he had seen it for himself. He took pains to keep his fellow ornithologists at arm's length and never discussed their work. They, in turn, hated him, and paid little attention to his work. Selous's habit of brushing off and isolating himself from other experts to concentrate on non-invasive interactions with birds might have been partly a reaction against his older brother, Frederick, a renowned weapons expert, whose big game hunts and glorious kills in South Africa had propelled him to fame. Despite the fact that Selous was solitary and withdrawn and his observations were barely acknowledged by his peers, he is considered to be the founder of field ornithology and his books on sexual and social behavior ushered in a paradigm shift in the ornithological world. He is a prime example of the benefits of independent thinking, a real game changer.

AND WE MUST remember that the increase in popularity of bird watching in its modern form would have been practically unthinkable without modern advances in technology. Changes in attitudes went hand in hand with changes in the equipment at people's disposal. Although binoculars existed from the middle of the nineteenth century, it was another half century before they were generally available. Then it became possible to take a closer look at birds without having to shoot them first. This, in turn, meant that people could turn their attention from what birds looked like to how they behaved. At first, only a few groups were enthusiastic about this new direction. Enter Edward Max Nicholson (1904–2003), who created a circle of students at the University of Oxford in 1926 who scoured the city and its environs for birds in their free time. The following year, Nicholson also published his first book, *The Birds of England,* which was followed in quick succession by *How Birds Live* and *The Art of Birdwatching.* It did not take long for the Oxford group to build up a good reputation, and in 1932, Nicholson founded the British Trust for Ornithology, which exists to this day. Later he entered the civil service, accompanying Winston Churchill to the conferences of Yalta and Potsdam. Despite his career as a bureaucrat, he remained a lifelong birder.

In addition to better binoculars with prismatic lenses and that almost silent mode of transportation, the bicycle, the camera also played a role in the increasing popularity of bird watching. *Bird Studies with a Camera* by Frank M. Chapman—the same Frank Chapman who introduced the Christmas Bird Count—became available in bookstores in 1900, and other books about bird watching soon followed. In many countries, bird watching developed into a grassroots movement, to some extent as a branch of nature study, which had already experienced an unprecedented boom in the second half of the nineteenth century. All this influenced the future of scientific investigation as old methods fell out of favor.

FEW EXPRESSED THEIR dissatisfaction with old-school, museum-based ornithology as unequivocally as the American Margaret Morse Nice (1883–1974):

> *I could see very little connection between the courses in college and the wild things I loved. I benefitted from the knowledge acquired of varied forms of life, but the approach to me seemed a dead one. I did not like to cut up animals.*

She made her mark in the world of scientific ornithology, where women's role had so far been mainly ornamental in nature. After the birth of her fourth child, Nice turned her attention to language development and wrote a book with her husband about the birds of Oklahoma. Although she had an MA in biology, she did not have a doctorate and often found herself obliged to explain, "I'm not a housewife, I am a trained zoologist." Eventually, she became widely known for her research into song sparrows. Her interactions with the leading lights of German ornithology in those days—Erwin Stresemann, Oskar Heinroth, and Konrad Lorenz—were particularly productive. And it is largely thanks to her that a network developed between some of the most important American and European ornithologists researching bird behavior. Ernst Mayr (1904–2005) played a key role in facilitating the connection. He had worked at the zoological museum in Berlin and collected birds for Lord Walter Rothschild in New Guinea before immigrating to the United States in 1931, where his first job was looking after the bird collection at the American Museum of Natural History in New York.

———————

IN THE EARLY days of the present century it was uncommon for ladies to tramp the moors looking for birds, or spend hours on cold winter days searching the shore for interesting waders or little-known ducks.

So read the obituary for Leonora Rintoul (1875–1953), and it was precisely these activities that were her passion—a passion shared by her friend Evelyn Baxter (1879–1959). Soon "the good ladies," as they were known, were some of the most influential experts on Scottish birds of their time. Every spring and fall from 1907 to 1933, they traveled 5 miles (8 kilometers) across the Firth of Forth to the Isle of May to observe migratory birds. Rintoul was said to be funny, warm, and motherly; Baxter was said to be reserved, capable, and somewhat intimidating. Together they presided over the Scottish Ornithologists' Club from its founding in 1936 until 1948.

KENN KAUFMAN IS the Jack Kerouac of birders. When the American entered the field, he started a new movement—or perhaps he picked up on something that was already in the air and simply set it into motion. By the 1960s, killing birds was an activity whose time had passed in ornithological circles, and collections were gradually beginning to gather dust. Shooting birds with guns was being replaced by shooting birds on film and, thanks to nature documentaries, viewers were now getting a glimpse of how birds lived in the wild. In the early 1970s, sixteen-year-old Kaufman, looking a bit like the popular image of Jesus, was hitchhiking to the farthest-flung reaches of the United States in search of birds. By the time he was eighteen, he had his sights set on recording the most North American birds seen in a single year—a concept now known as the Big Year. Local bird lovers came to his aid. One year he covered 6,900 miles (11,000 kilometers), sleeping under bridges, sometimes resorting to eating cat food, and earning a little by harvesting apples. When he was in Alaska, he could make out mountains in Siberia across the Bering Strait. During his travels, he encountered amazing characters among the bird watchers he met. For example, there was a young woman who identified so strongly with birds that she went by the name Peli.

Kaufman's restless activity far exceeded that of other birders traveling from continent to continent to check the boxes on their bird lists. As he explains in his book *Kingbird Highway,* he was driven not only by the desire to see as many birds as possible but also by the desire to understand them. By the end of his quest, in just one year, he had seen 630 of the 650 species of birds that reside on the North American continent. With that number, he exceeded even the legendary bird conservationist and founder of the famous

bird field guides, Roger Tory Peterson—who had encountered 572 species in 1953—and joined an elite group whose members had seen more than 600 birds in North America in one year. In the end, though, something happened that perhaps even he had not expected. He had a sudden change of heart and lost interest in bird lists. As he explained:

> *My big year started with a quest for a birding record but ended in a quest for something else…The most significant thing we find may not be the thing we are seeking. That is what redeems the crazy ambivalence of birding. As trivial as our listing pursuit may be, it gets us out there in the real world, paying attention, hopeful and awake. Any day could be a special day, and probably will be, if we just go out and look.*

What became paramount to him was no longer the numbers of birds he saw, but the birds themselves and how "birding cannot survive without birds." He (now joined by his wife, Kimberley) has made bird watching his life's work and has written numerous field guides to birds and birding.

IN ADDITION TO the concept of the Big Year, there is also the concept of a "life list"—a checklist of all the birds a bird watcher has seen over a lifetime. Both have their advocates. There are, of course, a limited number of people who have the means to fly from one region of the world to another to collect bird sightings. Some can do it because they have jobs that come with a high degree of mobility. An American named Peter G. Kaestner, for example, profited from his career as an international diplomat. He combined the travel he needed to do for work with his hobby, and he made the most of the opportunity. Kaestner is a life lister with a list of more than 8,500 species spotted. There are only a few people who have life lists longer than his. Tom Gullick, an 83-year-old Englishman, lists 9,096 species, although this number includes birds he has heard but not seen. With 9,414 species on his life list, fellow Englishman Jonathan Hornbuckle exceeds even Gullick's success. Hornbuckle confesses, with a touch of playfulness, to being "a victim of an obsession for birding," an activity, he says, that has given him much pleasure and a sense of purpose in life. Hornbuckle explains that he does not set out without knowing in advance which birds he wants to see. He takes a checklist along and works through it methodically. It seems, though, that Hornbuckle has his obsession at least somewhat under control, because he takes time on his travels to partake in important projects such as bird conservation and bird banding. Claes-Göran Cederlund, a Swedish doctor, lies just behind Hornbuckle. Long in Gullick's shadow, he has finally managed to overtake his rival—by 2016, he had a total of 9,169 bird species on his life list.

THERE ARE WEALTHY people who cut themselves off almost completely from their partners, children, and other family obligations to travel from one end of the world to the other for decades, often taking weeks-long journeys through trackless and dangerous regions in countries with sometimes dubious political regimes, where, on top of everything else, they then find themselves face to face with people who definitely do not have their best interests at heart. And all of this just to add one entry or another to a fervently kept list of bird sightings and to rise in the estimation of other twitchers (people who travel long distances just to catch a glimpse of a rare bird) and birders. Phoebe Snetsinger (1931–99), an American, was one of those people. Snetsinger had observed the occasional bird in the mid-1960s, but her unusually frenzied interest began after she was diagnosed with cancer in 1981 and told that she would not survive the year. Against all recommendations, she rejected any medical intervention and started taking high doses of vitamin C. Whereas other people in a similar situation might have decided to take life easy, she developed an extraordinary appetite for taking risks, which she often paired with a state of denial. After her diagnosis, she concentrated systematically and downright compulsively on spotting new species of birds around the globe. In other words, she turned into a hard-core birder.

As soon as she stepped on an airplane, she once explained, she was overcome with a feeling of being almost invincible and leaving all dangers behind her. In the early years, she recorded about a hundred new sightings with each journey—whether her travels took her to Brazil, Senegal, Malaysia, or Costa Rica. Later, the rate at which she added new sightings inevitably slowed down. During a trip to Papua New Guinea in 1984, she and her traveling companions found themselves on the sidelines of a tribal war. And yet she was soon writing that the journey had been "simply magnificent" and preferred to remember the twenty birds of paradise that she had observed there and the two hundred birds that she had been able to add to her list.

She did not get off so easily when she returned to this part of the world a year later. Out on the road, attackers forced her and the guide she was traveling with to a halt. Her guide suffered a machete wound and she was gang raped. As though she had already forgotten the incident that had almost cost her her life, she later said that she knew very well when she made the decision to track down birds around the world that there would be hard times. As Olivia Gentile highlights in her biography of Snetsinger, *Life List*, she never acknowledged that it might have been a bad decision to travel at a late hour with only her guide for company. In her own words:

> *I was unlucky, in one way, extremely fortunate to have escaped with my life in another. I have been [extraordinarily] fortunate in all my travels. The impact of the bastards in this world is a real threat—but it's not going to make me stay home & cringe in fear of doing what I've found to be the most rewarding pursuit of my life.*

Snetsinger died in a minibus accident in Madagascar in 1999 during a birding expedition, supposedly with binoculars in hand. She was sixty-eight years old. The last bird she spotted was the red-shouldered vanga, a small bird that had been described for science just two years earlier. She had seen 8,674 species, which is about 85 percent of all known bird species—a world record at the time of her death. She was a legend in her own lifetime, and her family continues the tradition: three of her four children have also dedicated their lives to birds.

MIGHT THERE BE a connection between being passionate about bird watching and being shy around people? Is it more than a coincidence that many people who have spent a long time being interested in birds withdraw and no longer function in society in ways that we expect? Since Snetsinger's death, the world of life listers and bird watchers has become much more accessible thanks to websites, blogs, and online forums. Like-minded people in just about every country can find each other and exchange tips online. They can broadcast almost in real time whenever a flock of rare birds is spotted. This online activity is an important method of monitoring what is happening with birds as a living, breathing component of Nature. In the meantime, in many countries, thousands of hobby ornithologists are mapping breeding ranges and counting waterfowl, acting as citizen scientists and making valuable contributions to work steered by professional ornithologists. This online chatter is a continuation of a drive to count and record that has been intensifying since the middle decades of the twentieth century.

Watching birds and taking notes is not just about numbers; these activities are also about writing history, telling stories, and holding out hope for the future. As Vernon R.L. Head wrote in *The Rarest Bird in the World*:

> *Each list is both a birdwatching past and a birdwatching future... Each name is a story of an interaction, a time of connection with the pristine, a collection of memories, an understanding of our place in the system of natural things, and a hope for the future of that place.*

It is difficult to say who or what was the impetus for these different ways of counting bird sightings. There was the annual Christmas Bird Count, of course, but the counts went way beyond that. Perhaps it was just a logical consequence of living in a world where the exhortation to go "faster, higher, farther" was becoming increasingly important, or maybe those who in other times might have become bird hunters needed to record their trophies in a different way. Maybe it was not so much a question of if it would happen but when. The increasing mathematical mania led to the founding of the American Birding Association in 1968. In contrast to the National Audubon Society, conservation was not front and center in this organization. According to the first edition of the association's newsletter, its primary motivation was to enjoy birds for hobby and "sport," and each issue of the newsletter was to include "the latest statistics on the various games that members are playing." The ultimate game was, of course, the race to spot birds.

Today, this might be a case of spotting the most bird species in a self-selected area within a twenty-four-hour period. Apart from possessing a great deal of stamina, the bird spotter needs to be able to recognize calls, plumage patterns, and the shapes of heads and beaks with lightning speed. Contrast this with the purpose of the Big Year, which is to see as many species of birds as possible in a calendar year. Big Years start on January 1 and may be limited to a county or a state, or may cover the entire North American continent. Mark Obmascik chronicled the many complications of this quirky endeavor for his 1998 book of the same name, which was made into a movie starring, among others, Steve Martin.

British ornithologist Dominic Couzens added a playful twist to the idea of "the most" and produced a list of "record" birds in his book *Extreme Birds*: the fastest bird (the peregrine), the bird with the longest toes (the northern jacana), the longest migration (the Arctic tern), the widest wingspan (the wandering albatross), the most feathers (the tundra swan), the longest egg incubation (emperor penguins), the largest egg in proportion to its body (the kiwi), the loudest call (the kakapo), the heaviest flier (the kori bustard, weighing in at nearly 50 pounds/22 kilograms), and so on.

TODAY, THERE ARE many different descriptions for people who love birds. Biologist Colin Tudge, who has spent four decades traveling the world, separates British birders into three categories:

The twitchers (known as listers in the United States), who are all about spotting as many birds as possible and adding to the list of birds they have seen. The birders (or bird watchers), who can spend days, weeks, or months observing birds, usually with no specific academic or professional goal in mind. And professional ornithologists. Meanwhile, a fourth category sometimes circulates among the company of bird lovers: the patchworker. Patchworkers cover territories ("patches") close to where they live, often confining their bird-watching efforts to their own gardens.

According to these definitions, Phoebe Snetsinger was a twitcher or lister, and English journalist Simon Barnes can be seen as an extreme form of birder:

> *I wasn't looking for birds, but I am always looking at them, you see... Looking at birds is a key: it opens doors, and if you choose to go through them you find you enjoy life more and understand life better... We humans tend to simultaneous and mutually exclusive desires: to be married, to be single; to be social, to be alone; to travel adventurously, to stay at home. Birdwatching embraces both halves of our natural desire for contradiction. It brings us enhanced enjoyment of the ordinary, the easy and the safe, and it brings us moments of high drama and gratification and dangerous delight.*

Some patchworkers are not satisfied with the confines of their own backyard, or maybe they do not even have one, and so they lay claim to a public park or open space near where they live. New York's Central Park is considered to be one of the most convenient places for bird watching anywhere in the United States. It seems paradoxical. There are often more birds out in the countryside, distributed more or less equally, but thanks to all the concrete and skyscrapers that surround it, the park is an oasis for birds, and because there are numerous grassy areas and the trees are more widely spaced in the park than they are out in the countryside, bird life here is less hidden and easier to observe than in untamed Nature. Since the park was established more than 150 years ago, 280 species of birds have been observed there—of which 192 are regular visitors and 88 drop by only occasionally or rarely. The crow and raven specialist John Marzluff spent a few hours in the park in 2013 and spotted 31 different species. Shortly before that, in Yellowstone National Park— that is to say, out in the wild far from any large urban center—a similar time period yielded only 24 species.

SARAH M. ELLIOTT must be one of the most frequent visitors to Central Park. She often spends up to twelve hours at a time there. Born in Chicago, this energetic-looking woman arrived in New York in the 1960s and soon made friends with the birds in the park. She counts them and scrupulously records their comings and goings. She even makes notes about the people who come to watch them. For decades, she has been leading those who are interested all over the park, for she knows every corner: "Oh! A winter wren! Now it's under the leaves. Now it's coming out! He's like a little round brown tennis ball. Now he's on the tree! Now he's behind the tree! Look at that tiny tail!"

Every once in a while Elliott sees really rare visitors flying by, and she is always hoping to be surprised. Once she saw a loon (a diver) taking a break on the reservoir, and she has seen golden eagles circling the Great Lawn apparently undeterred by the hubbub of the metropolis. Ospreys, and sometimes even bald eagles, are slightly more common. She loves showing people around, but she also loves being in the park alone, or almost so: "[The] best days, the magic days, are when you have a minute by yourself. That's when you feel the birds, and you feel the nature, and the trees. It all moves right in on you."

In fall, many migratory birds fly over the area, such as the pere-grine falcons making their way to South America after raising their young in nests on the MetLife high-rise nearby. The Audubon Soci-ety's annual Central Park Christmas Bird Count is always popular. In 2015, volunteers recorded 4,315 birds from 53 species. Elliott is just one of countless volunteers who are committed to leading simi-lar surveys all over the world.

A WORLD WHERE bird watchers dominate the discourse about birds raises questions about the relationship between ornithologists and lay people. In his book *A Passion for Birds,* Mark V. Barrow Jr. wrote, "As long as amateurs conformed to the scientists' expec-tations about what constitute the appropriate questions, methods, and results of research, university-trained ornithologists have gen-erally continued to welcome them into the field."

Environmental conditions for animals and plants are chang-ing as humans increasingly influence nature and the climate. And because of the importance of bird species as bio-indicators, bird watchers—amateurs and professionals alike—have an increasingly significant role to play in the future of the planet.

{ 16 }

Tracking Dodos
and Their Ilk

———

L ORD WALTER ROTHSCHILD (1868–1937) is generally known for his eccentric behavior, such as the time he drove to Buckingham Palace in a carriage pulled by zebras or when he rode on the back of a giant tortoise from the Galápagos. Perhaps less well known is that in 1892, this son of one of the most influential nineteenth-century Jewish bankers (a venture capitalist who made his fortune investing in diamonds and the Suez Canal) opened one of the most comprehensive private natural history museums in the world. His family kept birds—a tradition that continues today in the restored aviary at Waddesdon Manor, the family's one-time country home—and Rothschild developed his very own passion for these feathered creatures early in life.

At the tender age of ten, he created a small "museum" of stuffed birds in his bedroom and in a garden shed at the family estate in Tring. It later became the Walter Rothschild Zoological Museum, which contained, in addition to the mammals and reptiles in the collection, no fewer than 2,400 mounted birds, 300,000 skins, 200,000 eggs, and every other conceivable type of animal remains. Between 1890 and 1908, Rothschild had more than four hundred collectors scouring the world for him, and he also financed a handful of expeditions to places such as the Galápagos, Australia, and New Guinea. There was more to it than just purchasing the specimens, however. Experts were recruited to examine the offerings to see if they were authentic.

In 1904, Sir Walter Lawry Buller (1838–1906), one of the leading experts on the birds of New Zealand and author of a history of the birds of this island nation, offered Rothschild what appeared to be a rare adult white-faced laughing owl (a small bird that would go extinct about a decade later and that, despite its name, did not always come with white around the eyes). When Rothschild had the specimen checked out, he discovered that it was actually the head of a juvenile sewn onto the lower section of a different species. Accordingly, he refused to pay the agreed-upon price, which was a considerable sum, and spread word of the incident with great relish. Buller had provided Rothschild with hundreds of birds over the preceding fifteen years, and the incident was a great blow to his reputation.

While he was working in the family bank, Rothschild could only indulge in his hobby in the evenings and on weekends. It was 1908 before he managed to free himself from the bank's operations and devote himself to his collections at Tring. His curator was Ernst Hartert (1859–1933), one of the leading ornithologists of his day. As a young man, Hartert had tramped around the moors and marshes of Masuria, Poland, and taken part in an expedition to West Africa. Before he started work at Tring, he had traveled through numerous countries in Asia and South America—always on the trail of birds, butterflies, or beetles. Hartert had been hired by one of Rothschild's mentors, Albert Günther (1830–1914), a fish and bird expert of German extraction who had lived in England since 1858 and was

keeper of zoology at the British Natural History Museum. Günther had had a great deal of success breeding red-backed shrikes. For years, he spent his vacations at the seaside so his tame cormorants could go swimming.

Rothschild, who reportedly was very shy and had a bad stutter, was a compulsive collector and managed to become an authority on zoological matters despite a lack of formal education in the field. He was known for his phenomenal memory and supposedly could find each and every one of his beloved 300,000 bird skins without resorting to a catalog and could even describe their condition without needing to look at them. His collection of sixty-five stuffed cassowaries (flightless birds that are native to New Guinea and northern Australia), preserved in more or less natural postures, took up a great deal of space.

Apart from writing a book about bird life on Laysan, one of the northwestern Hawaiian Islands, Rothschild also wrote a large-format volume with a limited print run of just three hundred copies titled *Extinct Birds*. It was the very first book of its kind and the result of an enormous amount of diligent work. In the book, he described not only species of birds that had gone extinct within the preceding six or seven hundred years, but also a few more that, at the time Rothschild was writing his book, stood on the verge of extinction. (Rothschild was well aware that often the exact date of a bird's disappearance cannot be ascertained.) He included, in an appendix, sixty-three birds—for the most part flightless— whose appearance in many cases could only be guessed at based on remains and descriptions. Rothschild distinguished between birds "known externally as well as internally" and "those of which we know bones and egg-shells only." Not unexpectedly, the level of detail in the illustrations varied considerably.

Apart from the better known dodo, his "blue bird" is particularly striking. Decked out in blue feathers and a red bill, *Apterornis coerulescens* had been native to Réunion, a neighboring island of Mauritius. It had a body the size of a goose, but its feet were said to resemble those of a chicken. Rothschild wrote, "They do not fly at all, but run extremely quickly, so that a dog can hardly catch them; they are very good."

These birds, which according to what we know today would have belonged to the rail (or swamphen) family, clearly did not run away from their pursuers fast enough to save themselves from extinction. If this bird were alive today, it would be called the Réunion swamphen or *Porphyrio coerulescens*—as long as it was indeed a separate species. We will never know, but it might very possibly be identical to another bird we do know, the takahē or *Porphyrio hochstetteri*, which is also blue and flightless. The takahē was thought to be extinct in 1898, but it reappeared on the South Island of New

Rothschild's "blue bird"

Y

Zealand in 1948, the only place in the world where it can be found today.

One of the species Rothschild includes in his appendix comes with a story attached. In Rothschild's day, a number of collections contained specimens of the probably flightless *Traversia lyalli*—to which there are only two other references in scientific literature (one as *Xenicus insularis* and the other as *Traversia insularis*). The specimens all had one thing in common: they had all been dragged home by a cat called Tibbles that belonged to David Lyall, the lighthouse keeper on Stephens Island in New Zealand, a 600-acre (250-hectare) rocky island in Marlborough Sounds between the North and South islands.

"Evidently this feline discoverer has at the same time been the exterminator of *Traversia lyalli*, and many may have been digested by that unique cat." So reads Rothschild's sobering footnote. *Traversia lyalli* looks very much like a wren and has gone down in history as the Stephens Island wren, carrying the name of the island where it was last found. Rothschild believed that this little bird also used to exist on the main islands of New Zealand before it was exterminated there by rats and cats. Could it be that by writing about extinct birds, Rothschild was working through his fear of losing yet more of them?

Rothschild's relationship with money was complicated. In 1932, after being blackmailed, probably by a married mistress, he was forced to sell the majority of his bird skins to the American Museum of Natural History, turning it at one fell swoop into a museum with one of the most important bird collections in the world. Rothschild had to get rid of almost everything that he held dear and that was itself dear. He managed to keep only a small number of bird skins, including his beloved cassowaries, which are still on display at the museum in Tring. He also held onto some bird skeletons, nests, and, last but not least, his enormous collection of eggs.

AT ONE TIME, the passenger pigeon accounted for probably nearly half of the total number of birds on the North American continent. They had the unusual habit of gathering in gigantic flocks—until they were hunted as no bird had ever been hunted before. The tragic story is well known: the last of their kind, a bird by the name of Martha, died in the Cincinnati Zoo in 1914. For four years, visitors could go and stare at Martha, and occasionally throw sand at her to make her move. She had lost her partner, George, a couple of years earlier. After she fell off her perch, she was frozen into an enormous ice cube and transported to Washington, DC, and there, following strict protocols, dissected and stuffed. Since then she has haunted the Natural History Museum, sometimes here, sometimes there, a melancholy relic of an era long past.

Passenger pigeons were a particular interest of Paul Hahn (1875–1962), who was born in Reutlingen, Germany, moved with his parents to Canada when he was a boy, played the cello, and owned a successful piano dealership in Toronto. He soon became interested in birds, especially the passenger pigeon. Hahn got it into his head that he was going to find all the stuffed specimens of this extinct bird in private hands and donate them to the Royal Ontario Museum. He spent an unbelievable forty-five years tracking them down, and he was able to add the respectable number of sixty-eight specimens to the museum's collection. As time went on, he expanded his activities to a related area, making an inventory of authenticated specimens of other extinct birds (or birds that were presumed to be extinct) held in the collections of natural history museums around the world. In his book *Where Is That Vanished Bird?*, in addition to the passenger pigeon, he covered the Carolina parakeet, the ivory-billed woodpecker, the great auk, the dodo, the Labrador duck, and the Eskimo curlew.

But perhaps the passenger pigeon has only temporarily disappeared from our planet? Ben Novak, of the Californian Long Now

Foundation, has resolved to sequence the genome of the bird in order to resurrect it. He has taken tissue samples from thirty-four skins he found in a variety of natural history collections. His goal is to generate the passenger pigeon's primordial germ cells, which would then be implanted in chicken embryos or the embryos of related pigeon species. If these birds mature and multiply, which is what Novak and his colleagues are hoping for, at some point the wished-for pigeons will come into being. Novak stresses that it will be a very long time before billions of them once again darken the sky. Whether that is even desirable is a question that has yet to be answered.

THE DODO—A STRANGE-LOOKING giant pigeon whose name likely comes from the Portuguese word *doido,* meaning "crazy"—is another bird that lives on only in the collective imagination. Finnish photographer Harri Kallio staged the resurrection of this bird, which went extinct before the invention of photography. He took specially constructed models to the birds' former habitat in Mauritius and reconstructed scenes modeled on the birds' imagined life. A bizarre project, when you consider that there is not a single skin in existence and all speculation about the bird's physical appearance is based on a few bones found in a Mauritian swamp. Recent research suggests that dodos had longer legs than and were not as plump as generally thought, but it will be quite some time before the stereotypical image fades away. The idea that the dodo was a stocky, roundish bird can be traced back to the Dutch painter Roelandt Savery, mentioned earlier in this book, who sketched live dodos he saw in the menagerie of Maurice, Prince of Orange. The project invokes a strange sense of melancholy, for—whatever the birds might really have looked like—you are left with the feeling that no matter how technically accurate the reconstruction, it can never be more than a pale reflection of the creature itself.

TIM GALLAGHER IS an American author and photographer who works at the Cornell Laboratory of Ornithology. The object of his desire is the ivory-billed woodpecker, a graceful bird with black-and-white plumage, a red crest, and an ivory-colored bill. Gallagher's interest in the bird dates back to the early 1970s, when he read an article in *Time* magazine in which the author claimed to have spotted the bird in Big Thicket, an area of dense forest and waterways in southeast Texas. At the time, the bird was believed to be extinct, and scientists soon cast doubt on the author's claim. The last authenticated sighting of the North American subspecies was by Don Eckelberry, who managed to get some snapshots of the bird in April 1944. (The last substantiated sighting of the Cuban subspecies was in 1987.)

According to Gallagher, not only does the ivory-billed woodpecker have size, beauty, and a sense of mystery, it is also "a symbol of everything that has gone wrong with our relationship to the environment." He wrote:

> *I thought that if someone could just locate an ivory-bill, could prove that this remarkable species still exists, it would be the most hopeful event imaginable: we would have one final chance to get it right, to save this bird and the bottomland swamp forests that it needs to survive.*

Not unexpectedly, his passion was reignited when a turkey hunter reported that he had seen a pair of ivory-billed woodpeckers in a swamp in Louisiana in spring 1999. The report unleashed an unprecedented search: for obscure sources in the ornithological literature; for people who claimed to have seen the bird; and, of course, for the bird itself. Finally, Gallagher traveled to various swampy areas in the southern United States where he thought the bird might be. The search culminated on February 27, 2004, with the sighting of a bird with the characteristic white patterning on its otherwise black wings. This sighting led to the 2005 publication of a three-page article in *Science* that had no fewer than seventeen co-authors. The article led to one of the most heated debates in ornithological history.

The claim that the bird still existed polarized American bird lovers. The bone of contention was a blurry, out-of-focus photograph that had been produced as proof of the sighting. Where exactly was the distinctive white trailing edge of the bird's wing? A fraction of those who saw the photograph thought they could identify the hoped-for ivory-billed woodpecker; the rest saw "only" the pileated woodpecker, which is widely distributed in North America and is not threatened with extinction, and whose population is actually on the rise. The following year, another article in *Science* refuted Gallagher's findings. As of 2016, the debate continues, as does the search for the bird.

After that, Gallagher transferred his interest to another bird. He began searching for the imperial woodpecker instead. Standing up to 2 feet (60 centimeters) tall, it is the largest woodpecker in the world. Native to Mexico, it is considered to be the ivory-billed woodpecker's closest relative. The starting point was similar to the one for its North American relative. The last sighting had been more

than half a century earlier and there had been no reliable documentation since 1956; however, there were persistent rumors circulating among the residents of mountain villages in the western Sierra Madre that the bird still existed in remote areas. Gallagher wanted to find out for sure whether the rumors were correct. He realized this would be no easy undertaking, but there turned out to be substantial challenges due to circumstances that took him completely by surprise, as Gallagher explained when he wrote to me.

> *Unfortunately, this region is the epicenter of illegal drug growing (both opium poppies and marijuana) in Mexico, and in my travels I had several dangerous encounters with armed narcotraficantes. I launched five expeditions in search of this bird, and each time the situation seemed 100 times worse. On my final expedition, it seemed more like being in the mountains of Afghanistan than Mexico, with armed men, burning houses, and fleeing villagers, and I felt grateful to escape with my life.*

Perhaps in reaction to these experiences in a completely alien environment, Gallagher decided to set off once more in search of the ivory-billed woodpecker—and also to celebrate the tenth anniversary of its supposed first sighting since its reported demise. No one has the right to put a damper on his zeal, but does the obstinate search for the ivory-billed woodpecker have any "real" point beyond settling the question of whether the bird still exists or not? The British naturalist Mark Cocker makes a persuasive argument when he suggests that the search for the bird "has acquired elements of a religious myth or parable, encompassing the notions of mortal sin but also of collective redemption through the bird's rediscovery."

YOU COULD SAY the story of the starling is the exact opposite of the story of the passenger pigeon. With its iridescent metallic green- or purple-colored feathers, the starling is a striking bird to look at. It also has a distinctive, piercing call. Wolfgang Amadeus Mozart had a starling that has gone down in history. Starl came into Mozart's life on May 2, 1784. Starl was obviously a quick study and could chirp his own rendition of his master's compositions. When the bird died three years later, the composer is said to have been so grief-stricken that he orchestrated a procession of heavily veiled mourners and composed a farewell poem. Reportedly, the loss of his bird affected him more deeply than the death of his father, Leopold, who passed away the same week—although some researchers dispute this.

Starlings are not native to the North American continent. They arrived thanks to an unusual excursion into classical literature. Drug manufacturer and philanthropist Eugene Schieffelin (1827–1906) wanted to introduce starlings to the United States because they make an appearance in one of Shakespeare's plays. (A starling is mentioned in *Henry IV*, Part 1, Act 1, Scene 3.) Schieffelin was a member of the American Acclimatization Society, founded in 1871, whose mission was to introduce foreign animals and plants that were either useful or interesting. They had the odd idea that the indigenous flora and fauna was incomplete, and they wanted to introduce the ones they missed from the Old World.

On a snowy day in March 1890, Schieffelin released one hundred starlings for the first time in New York's Central Park. He did the same thing the following year. He supposedly tried to introduce another forty species, all of which eventually disappeared from the area. A decade after Schieffelin's actions, in 1900, the Lacey Act was passed, which included a ban on introducing non-native animals into the United States. Under this act, what Schieffelin did would have been illegal. Since then, the couple of hundred starlings he released have multiplied to form an army many millions strong.

{ 17 }

Recording Nature

BIRDSONG IS COMPLEX. Despite a great deal of research, much remains a mystery, including whether "song" is even the right term to categorize the sounds birds make. Humans are quick—perhaps too quick—to judge the characteristic qualities of birdsong solely according to its aesthetic appeal. When it comes to hearing, people and birds not only respond to a different, albeit overlapping, range of frequencies, but also perceive certain sounds in a qualitatively different way. Beyond that, many acoustic details are lost to us when we break down birds' vocal expressions into their individual components and focus on their audio frequencies. The anthropomorphic interpretation of these sounds as "song" suggests that birds produce these sounds for pleasure; however, there are other, more obvious, reasons for vocalizing, such as defending territory or attracting a mate. According to recent research, the accuracy with which a bird can repeat certain patterns of sound might signal the bird's physical condition and its fitness as a mate. The attempt to translate bird sounds and "melodies" into meaningful human speech patterns is, quite simply, impossible.

NOT EVERYONE HAS the ability to mimic birds, but a little practice can go a long way. You need both acute hearing and vocal skill.
Englishman Percy Edwards (1908–96) was well known for both. He
was a frequent guest on radio shows and could imitate the sounds
of six hundred different birds, as well as other animals, including whales, reindeer, and sheep. He was not only a much-loved
entertainer, but also a recognized ornithologist. Luis F. Baptista
(1942–2000)—a famous bioacoustics expert who was born in Hong
Kong and grew up in Macao but spent most of his life in the United
States—could imitate numerous birds from Alaska to Costa Rica
and soon became known as the "maestro of the avian symphony."
He championed the idea that certain birds even create dialects, and
he believed he could identify where white-crowned sparrows were
from thanks to differences in their songs. He also talked of bilin-
gual or trilingual birds. Once when he was out in Presidio Park in
San Francisco making recordings with his parabolic reflector, he
was arrested on suspicion of being a Communist spy.

WHEN IT BECAME technically possible to record the sounds birds
made, new horizons opened up for bird lovers. It is certainly no accident that musicians were among the pioneers here. One example
is the German violinist and singer Ludwig Koch (1881–1974), who
devised special recording equipment to take along when he accompanied ornithologists out into songbirds' territories. He made his
first recordings with an Edison wax-cylinder phonograph when he
was a boy, and he was one of the first people to notice the spread of
the collared dove in Europe after the 1930s. After immigrating to
England in 1936, he continued his work in the form of books and
radio programs, and established himself as the European pioneer of
recording wild birds in their natural surroundings.

Albert R. Brand (1889–1940), one of Koch's contemporaries,
worked as a trader on the New York Stock Exchange before going

Ludwig Koch

out into the countryside, armed with cumbersome equipment he had developed himself, to record bird sounds. The recordings he and his colleagues made at the end of the 1920s are the basis for the audio archive at Cornell University, the Macaulay Library, which is now the world's leading scientific collection of biodiversity media. After writing a book about wild bird songs, in the late 1930s, Brand produced an entire album of American bird songs. The Albert R. Brand Bird Song Foundation was set up in his name.

THERE ARE A great number of musicians who have birdsong to thank for their inspiration and who work it into their compositions in every conceivable way. The birdsongs in the first scene of *Der Rosenkavalier* (The Knight of the Rose) by Richard Strauss come

Albert Brand's equipment being used in the field

to mind, or Ludwig van Beethoven's *Pastoral Symphony* with its bird calls, where yellowhammers, quail, nightingales, and cuckoos apparently helped with the composition (though this is debatable as it's more likely he wrote the piece at his desk in Vienna than at a desk on the banks of a woodland stream). *Gli Uccelli* (The Birds), a baroque suite for strings by the Italian composer Ottorino Respighi, features movements marked as "The Hen," "The Nightingale," "The Dove," and so on. And the last two minutes of the third movement of the symphonic poem *Pini di Roma* (Roman Pines) include bird sounds—on a clear night under a full moon, a nightingale is singing in the branches of a pine.

French composer Olivier Messiaen (1908–92) was encouraged early on by one of his teachers to listen to birds. He collected birdsongs from many different parts of the world, which he incorporated into his work. He considered his transcriptions of birdsongs to be "absolutely true to life." *Le merle noir* (The Blackbird), composed for flute and piano, is based on the blackbird's song. *Réveil des oiseaux* (The Birds Awaken), a piece for full orchestra, is courtesy of the birds you can hear between midnight and midday in the Jura Mountains in France. Finally, Messiaen's piece *Oiseaux exotiques* (Exotic Birds), for piano and small orchestra, offers the voices of little-known birds from distant lands. Messiaen was a devout Catholic, and for him, birds received their gift from God and were the most talented musicians in the world. Messiaen, for his part, might not have been the ornithologist he claimed to be, but he was a wonderful composer.

Inspired by Chinese and Asian pigeon whistles in the collection at the Pitt Rivers Museum, Oxford, artist and composer-in-residence Nathaniel Mann created a kinetic multimedia piece involving a flock of specially trained Birmingham roller pigeons. He built his own pigeon whistle using a cut-down plastic 35-mm film canister, a couple of ice-pop sticks, and a sliver of a broken record. He built fifteen whistles, each capable of producing a different note, and each pigeon had a whistle attached to its tail feathers. As soon as the birds took flight, air drawn through the whistles produced a cluster of tones—celestial music, if you will.

The American musician-philosopher-engineer-professor David Rothenberg appears a little out of step with the times, although in a unique and charming way. It could even be that he is not so much out of step with the times as striding out ahead of them. For fifteen years, he has been making music in the company of birds, considering them not as colorful background performers but as active collaborators in composition:

> *Playing with birds, rather than merely thinking about birds, I begin to feel what it is like to be a bird. I do not look for proof but only possibility, and hope for new ways to interact, new sounds to surprise. Wild things.*

The result, according to Rothenberg, is nothing less than a unique "inter-species interaction." He goes one step further and suggests that birds might reciprocate these feelings: "Those people, they don't just cage us and feed us and listen to us—maybe they're ready to learn from us too."

Rothenberg is particularly enchanted by the extremely complex song of the nightingale. He hopes that one day, by using a combination of musical and biological approaches—art and science—he will come closer to understanding and perhaps even to deciphering it.

I had the opportunity to meet with Rothenberg in a café in Berlin. When I asked him what was special about making music with birds, he said:

> *One is playing with a creature who only has music, not language, so perhaps their music means far more to them than it could ever mean to us. And one dares to try to communicate across species lines, using*

the very logic and emotion of life itself, the emotional shapes and forms that evolution has provided millions of years before humans ever appeared on this planet. It's a sobering thought.

DAVID ROTHENBERG WAS not the first person to play music with birds, or at least to assume that this was what he was doing. In the 1920s, a British cellist named Beatrice Harrison (1892–1965) developed the charming habit of going out into her large garden in Surrey in southeast England in the spring to practice playing music.

As the nights began to feel warmer I had a sudden longing to go out into the woods surrounding the garden and play my cello and gaze on the beauty of it all as the moon peeped out through the trees. I sat on an old seat which surrounded an ivy-clad tree. I began to play, very lazily, all the melodies I loved best and to improvise on them. I began the Chant hindou *by Rimsky-Korsakov and after playing for some time I stopped. Suddenly a glorious note echoed the notes of the cello. I then trilled up and down this instrument, up to the top and down again: the voice of the bird followed me in thirds! I had never heard such a bird's song before—to me it seemed a miracle. The sound did not appear to come from the high treetops but from nearer the ground; I could not see, I just played on and on.*

After hearing the nightingale joining in and responding with trills of its own, Harrison proposed performing this "collaborative" performance live on the radio. The British Broadcasting Corporation (BBC) accepted her offer with alacrity. The technical challenges were considerable, as whole truckloads of equipment had to be delivered. She played on May 19, 1924, a warm, clear, moonlit night—sitting on a stone bench next to the bush where the bird was perched—to several million listeners. For a long time, the bird did not join in, and the radio program was coming to an end (almost two hours had passed by then) when suddenly, after Harrison had begun Antonín Dvořák's *Songs My Mother Taught Me,* the nightingale sang—or at least reacted. The audience's response was overwhelming. The BBC had pulled off a coup, and news of the performance spread around the globe. Thanks to their great success, the concerts were repeated every spring for the next twelve years. In 1942, the BBC planned a live broadcast of the nightingale singing alone, but as they set up their equipment, British bombers began to fly overhead on their way to Europe. The engineers realized a live broadcast would compromise the military operation, so they recorded the session instead—capturing the sounds of 197 Wellington and Lancaster bombers flying out on a raid over Mannheim, and the sounds of 11 fewer planes returning as the nightingale sang on into the night. To this day, there are doubts about the interactions between the musician and the bird. Was it pure fantasy to think that the bird was singing in response to the sound of the cello? Perhaps the whole thing was nothing more than a charming coincidence.

{ 18 }

Deadly Obsessions

WHEN PEOPLE CHASE birds, sometimes it is not only the birds that are at risk. Quite a few hunters have paid for their greed for avian plunder with their lives. Some succumbed to wild animal attacks or to insidious tropical diseases. For example, in 1910, Captain Boyd Alexander—who had trained his sights on the birdlife of the Cape Verde islands, the islands in the Gulf of Guinea, and the Gold Coast, as well as West and Central Africa—was beaten to death by a mob of hostile villagers and soldiers in Chad. Gustav Garlepp—who had previously collected birds in the Amazon and in Bolivia—was robbed and killed by his porters in the Andes in 1907. There are many reports of an errant shot that wounded an unsuspecting hunter or even sent him to his death. Occasionally the route to death was more circuitous. Erich Hummitzsch (1904–69) from Saxony, who had banded fifteen thousand birds over the course of three decades, succumbed to gas poisoning when he tried to climb up a large gas tank from the inside in order to observe kestrels. Baron Christoph von Biedermann (1862–1913), who owned twenty-four falcons and must have known a great deal about them—although he never managed to consolidate all his knowledge into a book—was carried off after five long years of suffering the effects of a blood infection from an injury to his eye that one of his falcons had inflicted with a talon.

According to the *Guinness Book of Records*, the cassowary is the most dangerous of all birds, for both people and their pets. It cannot fly, but it can move at a speed of up to 30 miles (50 kilometers) an hour and jump a full 3 feet (1 meter) up into the air. It pecks at windshields, runs after cars, and will even take on a terrier. It boasts three toes on each foot; the middle toe is shaped like a scimitar and is just as sharp. In 1926 in Queensland, Australia, sixteen-year-old Philip McLean had his throat slit open by a cassowary when he tried to kill the bird. Although there have been no fatalities recorded since then, there are numerous other documented cases of broken ribs or legs after altercations with the birds or of ugly wounds inflicted by them. Ironically, the majority of accidents with cassowaries happen when people are trying to feed them.

Birds like to lay their eggs in places that are difficult to reach, not only for potential animal predators but also for humans. John C. Caboon, a well-known collector and trader in Massachusetts, had been stalking birds for fifteen years. In 1891, a few years after he had hit the headlines with news of his hazardous collecting expeditions on the coastal cliffs of Newfoundland, he lowered himself down 200 feet (60 meters) of precipitous cliff to reach four eggs from a raven's nest. On the climb back up, he foundered at an overhang and fell, completely exhausted, to a watery death.

A decade later, a tragic fate befell Francis J. Birtwell in 1901. After falling ill with tuberculosis, the former Harvard University student moved to the arid American Southwest. One day, he was collecting eggs at the top of a 65-foot (20-meter) pine for his thesis research and panicked when a gust of wind hit. He called for help,

and his young wife and a group of men threw him a rope so that he could lower himself down. Unfortunately, as he tried to descend, a knot in the rope caught on a branch, and Birtwell fell 30 feet (10 meters) toward the ground. As he tried to free himself, the rope slipped from under his arm to around his neck and, tragically, he was hanged.

Curiosity about birds was the cause of the grisly death of the experienced bird guide David Hunt in 1985. His last tour took him to Corbett National Park in India, in the foothills of the Himalayas—for the umpteenth time. After he had told his group of eighteen travelers to continue on to the tour bus, which was standing there ready and waiting for them, he set out on a side path. Reports differ on the details of what happened next, although the photographs on his camera provide some clues. The first photograph shows a spotted little owl sitting on a branch. The next shows a tiger approaching the photographer. The close-up of bared teeth in the final photograph anticipates the tragic outcome. The incident played out within seconds, and the group heard an ear-splitting shriek. His autobiography, *Confessions of a Scilly Birdman* (pronounced "silly," a play on

The pursuit of birds—some real, some existing only in the imagination—could be deadly.

the name of the place he was from, the British Isles of Scilly), was published only after his death.

To be in the wrong place at the wrong time does not always lead to a fatal outcome, of course. The British ornithologist Stephanie Tyler got off if not lightly, then at least with her life. In 1976, during an expedition to northern Ethiopia with her husband and her two children, she was attacked by rebels and held hostage for eight months before being released unharmed. The only loss she complained about later was the loss of her telescope. Other than that, she was able to put her time as a hostage to good use—watching birds.

{ 19 }

Fantasies of Flight

WHAT WOULD IT be like to swim up into an ocean of air like a bird? Along with all the stories about avian enthusiasms, there is a long list of philosophical reflections and practical experiments devoted to realizing this fantasy. In ancient mythology, these go as far back as the story of Icarus, who flew too close to the sun, melting the wings his father, Daedalus, had fashioned for him out of feathers and wax, and plunging to his death in the sea. Stories about spending time in the ethereal realm generally assumed that stays were temporary and were shot through with ambivalent feelings about the element itself and moral concerns about its suitability as a place for human beings to be. After all, there were not only angels in the firmament, but also ghosts and witches, and sometimes the sky rained stones or frogs. Wouldn't God have given people wings if he had wanted them to fly?

Leonardo da Vinci (1452–1519) is the most prominent person from the Renaissance to have thought about flight, and he was the first person to approach the subject from a scientific perspective. He

took great delight in birds, and Giorgio Vasari, famous court painter to the Medici family, once spotted him buying them at the market solely to set them free.

After carefully considering both birds and bats, da Vinci was inspired to outfit a complicated flying machine he had designed with wings modeled on bat wings because he decided feathered wings would be too difficult to recreate artificially. He documented most of his experiments in *Codex on the Flight of Birds,* subdividing his notes thematically into flight driven by wing power, gliding, the flight of insects, animals, and fish, and building a flying machine. As a precaution, in case any officers of the Inquisition paid him a visit, he wrote the text in mirror writing.

He was of the opinion that birds increase the density of the air beneath them when they beat their wings, creating something like a pillow that they can fly on. He might not have been right about that, but he was right when he realized that a flying object must encounter wind resistance and should therefore be constructed as aerodynamically as possible. Da Vinci thought the main problem with flight lay in maintaining balance. Astoundingly, he thought that human strength alone was sufficient for winged flight. To make take-off and landing easier, he envisioned stilts, which would also help lessen the impact if the machine crashed. He advised testing any machine over water, "so that in case of a crash you don't hurt yourself." And he advised flying above the clouds so that the wings did not get wet and so there was enough time to right the machine if it rolled over. How the flier would get up that high in the first place da Vinci did not say.

MORE THAN A hundred years after da Vinci, the Neapolitan physicist Giovanni Alfonso Borelli (1608–79), who was a pioneer in the field of biomechanics and corresponded with members of the Royal Society in London, had some further thoughts about bird flight. In his book *De motu animalium* (On the Movement of Animals), which appeared after his death in 1685, he explained the anatomical structure of the wing and applied mathematical principles to explain its movement, which touched off an animated storm of discussion among learned experts in Europe. He saw birds converting their God-given geometry into flight. His main proposition was that wings acted like wedges to part the air. He resisted the idea championed by Aristotle that a bird's tail functioned like a rudder on a

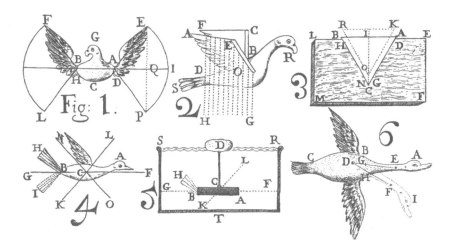

ship. The only function of the tail, as far as he was concerned, was to guide movement up or down; he did not see it working on a horizontal plane to move the bird left or right. He also reckoned that the muscle birds needed to beat their wings made up one-sixth of their body mass, whereas the arm and chest muscles in a human being were less than one-hundredth of their total mass. And with that, Borelli robbed people of their illusion that they would ever achieve human-powered flight. Their chest muscles were simply not strong enough.

BUT JUST BECAUSE something is physically impossible does not mean that people give up on the idea completely. In *Historia Antigua de México* (Ancient History of Mexico), first published in 1780/81, Francisco Javier Clavijero wrote about a remarkable "experiment in flight."

> *They looked for a very tall tree in the woods, cut off the branches and the bark, brought it into the town, and erected it in a large square on the hill. They stuck the top of the tree into a wooden cylinder that the Spanish called a mortar, because that is what it looked like. From this cylinder hung four stout ropes that served to support a square. Between the cylinder and the square four more stout ropes were attached, which were wrapped around the tree for as many times as the fliers were to rotate around it. These four ropes were passed through four holes made in the four poles that made the square. The four best fliers, dressed as eagles, herons, and other birds, climbed very quickly up the tree using a rope that had been slung around it reaching from the ground to the square. From the square, they climbed, one at a time up to the cylinder. And after they had danced around up here for a short time, they wrapped the ends of the ropes that went through the holes in the square around themselves. Now each leapt down and began their flight using their outspread wings.*

The movement of their bodies set the cylinder and the square in motion. Gradually the square unwound the ropes on which the fliers were swinging down as it rotated. As the ropes were now getting longer, they were tracing bigger and bigger circles as they flew. While these four were flying circuits around the tree, a fifth up above on the cylinder beat on a small drum or waved a flag without showing the slightest concern about falling off. As soon as the others on the square, where usually ten to twelve people were standing, saw that the fliers had completed their last circuit, they descended helter-skelter down to the ground on those same ropes to the applause of the people who had gathered to watch.

It is not clear whether jumping off the complicated and striking structure actually gives any feel for what it means to fly. These dances were traditionally performed by the Totonacs, an indigenous people from Central Mexico. Today the "fliers" are known as the *Voladores de Papantla* (The Fliers of Papantla), and they execute their ritual aerial display as a tourist attraction.

Until well into the nineteenth century, all kinds of people were wracking their brains over the ground rules of flight mechanics. Bird flight was still a long way from being understood, and people had only a vague idea about the principles of aerodynamics. How can you overcome gravity? Balloons, it seems, prove the maxim "lighter than air," even if all they do is soar upward and float. As the belief in human muscle power wasted away, so did the production of all those fancifully designed flying machines. People turned to gunpowder, carbon dioxide, air pressure, and—eventually—gasoline as a means of propulsion. An important part of the efforts from then on were directed toward aircraft. None of the research or experiments changed the fact that people, with the bodies they had, would never be able to fly unless they had help.

Epilogue

B IRD WATCHING IS only one of many ways to get involved with
birds. Falconry and pigeon breeding go back millennia. In
ancient times, there were the first careful experiments to try
to understand bird anatomy and to find out how birds worked. As
new continents were discovered by explorers from the West, many
hitherto unknown birds were also discovered and the evolving discipline of natural sciences had to come up with a new understanding
of the natural world and a new way to classify its contents. Eager
collectors served the public's growing interest in birds. The first
public collections and natural history museums were established.
Soon people were no longer content to view stuffed birds and bird
skins; they filled their menageries with living specimens and decorated their drawing rooms with cage-birds. At the beginning of the
nineteenth century, ornithology emerged as a scientific discipline
in its own right. The revolution in biology and insights into evolution were closely associated with research into the bird world. By
the end of the nineteenth century, when it became clear that human

intervention in the natural world posed a danger for bird populations, people began to realize that birds needed to be protected. The
bird conservation movement, which united citizens and scientists,
is today one of the strongest conservation movements of all. Using
all the technical means at its disposal, it identifies alarming environmental impacts and works to halt population decline.

Millions of people are involved. The army of bird conservationists overlaps with the army of bird watchers, who often find their
way to the farthest reaches of the planet. Fifty million people in the
United States today consider themselves to be birders. We are living
in a time of birdmania. Such interest is unprecedented. Although
historically birds have not benefitted from the interest people have
shown in them, today this interest holds the key to extricating ourselves from the situation in which we now find ourselves. We have to
come to terms with the paradox that although we know more than
ever about birds, we are also watching more and more species head
toward extinction. One-eighth of the species alive today are in danger of disappearing in the near future.

In this book, we have reacquainted ourselves with or, perhaps,
met for the first time, people who are known to varying degrees and
who, in one way or another, were or are interested in birds. Let us
gently remind ourselves in closing that many people manifest their
interest in birds, or simply enjoy them, with little fuss or fanfare.
Think, for example, of the many people who make the colder seasons of the year a little easier for birds in their garden by putting
out food or whose gardens are full of seeds and insects that birds
delight in, or walkers and hikers who enjoy birds without having
the slightest intention of observing their behavior or even making a
note of their encounters.

While working on the final pages for this book, I came across
an unusual example of a human–bird relationship—and maybe even
an example of coevolution. In Mozambique, there is a bird called a

honeyguide that has likely evolved with humans over thousands of years. Both the Yao and the birds are on the trail of bee nests—the birds for the wax, which is a good source of calories for them, and the people for the honey. It is unclear who has trained whom, but when the human bee hunters make a particular sound—a combination of a trill followed by a grunt—the birds arrive. Alternatively, the birds seek out the bee hunters by flying close to them and shrieking. Whoever makes the first move, the partners are now ready to go. Thanks to their well-developed sense of smell, the birds know where the nests are, but they cannot get past the aggressive bees to get the wax. The people have difficulty finding the nests, but once they have located one, they know how to smoke out the bees and then chop down the tree to get at it safely. When they drain out the honey, they leave the wax for the birds. Some scientists even wonder whether easy access to energy-rich honey helped humans increase the size of their brains. Might a small bird have played a role in the evolution of modern humans? The idea is intriguing. In the meantime, the story of the Yao and their honeyguides is a tale of humans and birds bound together to survive.

Acknowledgments

I N 2015, MY book about people who are passionate about birds was published in Germany. I would like to thank Rob Sanders, publisher of Greystone Books, for taking an interest and exploring how best to adapt it for the English-language market. We soon agreed on revising the German text and illustrating it with vintage artwork. Jane Billinghurst then made most helpful suggestions for the revisions and did an admirable job of both editing and translating the text into English. The contributions of the copy editor, Lesley Cameron, were invaluable, and the stellar design crew at Greystone (most especially Nayeli Jimenez) put the elements together into a most attractive package. The process reminded me that a book is a collaborative effort involving author, editor, translator, designer, and publisher, and all the people who work to bring it to market.

A number of other people provided support and answered my queries. Many thanks to Mark V. Barrow Jr., Carla Dove, Jonathan Franzen, Tim Gallagher, Helmut Laußmann, Helen Macdonald, John Marzluff, David Rothenberg, Frank Steinheimer, Scott

Weidensaul, and a dear friend who prefers to remain unnamed here. Any problems that remain are, of course, my responsibility.

Martina Rißberger and Hans-Ulrich Raake of the library of the Museum für Naturkunde—Leibniz Institute for Evolution and Biodiversity Science, Berlin, were very helpful in finding most of the vintage illustrations in this book. I would also like to thank the museum for giving me permission to reproduce the illustrations here.

My gratitude also extends to Susanne Rolf-Dietrich, scout for Greystone Books in Germany; to Markus Hoffmann, partner at Regal Hoffmann & Associates; to Wolfgang Hörner, my publisher of the German edition; and to the many artists of former centuries who unknowingly (and hopefully not unwillingly, had they known) contributed to making this volume so visually appealing.

Last but not least, I would like to thank Riky Stock and the German Book Office New York and also New Books in German for selecting this book and helping with a grant to translate it into English.

Selected Bibliography and Sources for Quotes

This bibliography lists the books I found most useful
or fascinating when I did my research.

Ackerman, Jennifer. *The Genius of Birds*. New York: Penguin, 2016.

Baker, J.A. *The Peregrine*. New York: Harper & Row, 1967.

Barnes, Simon. *How to Be a (Bad) Birdwatcher*. New York: Pantheon Books, 2005.

Barrow, Mark V., Jr. *A Passion for Birds: American Ornithology after Audubon*. Princeton: Princeton University Press, 1998.

Baynes, Ernest Harold. *Wild Bird Guests: How to Entertain Them*. New York: E. P. Dutton & Company, 1915.

Bechstein, Johann Matthäus. *The Natural History of Cage Birds: Their Management, Habits, Food, Diseases, Treatment, Breeding, and the Methods of Catching Them*. London: H.J. Drane, 1837.

Berlepsch, Hans Freiherr, von. *Der gesamte Vogelschutz, seine Begründung und Ausführung*. Gera-Untermhaus: Eugen Köhler Verlag, 1899.

Birkhead, Tim. *The Wisdom of Birds: An Illustrated History of Ornithology.* London: Bloomsbury, 2008.

——— *Bird Sense: What It's Like to Be a Bird.* London: Bloomsbury, 2012.

Birkhead, Tim, Jo Wimpenny, and Bob Montgomerie. *Ten Thousand Birds: Ornithology since Darwin.* Princeton: Princeton University Press, 2014.

Bowles, Paul. *Travels: Collected Writings, 1950–1993.* London: Sort of Books, 2010.

Brehm, Alfred E. *Das Leben der Vögel.* Glogau: Verlag Carl Flemming, 1861.

Büchner, Ludwig. *Liebe und Liebes-Leben in der Thierwelt.* Berlin: Hofmann & Co., 1879.

Burtt, Edward H., Jr. *Alexander Wilson: The Scot Who Founded American Ornithology.* Cambridge: Harvard University Press, 2013.

Chansigaud, Valérie. *All about Birds: A Short Illustrated History of Ornithology.* Princeton: Princeton University Press, 2010.

——— *Des hommes et des oiseaux.* Paris: Delachaux et Niestlé, 2012.

Cocker, Mark, and David Tipling. *Birds and People.* London: Jonathan Cape, 2013.

Conniff, Richard. *The Species Seekers: Heroes, Fools, and the Mad Pursuit of Life on Earth.* New York: W. W. Norton & Co., 2011.

Couzens, Dominic. *Extreme Birds: The World's Most Extraordinary and Bizarre Birds.* Richmond Hill: Firefly Books, 2011.

Cruickshank, Helen. *Thoreau on Birds.* New York: McGraw-Hill, 1964.

D'Albertis, L.M. *New Guinea: What I Did and What I Saw.* London: Sampson Low, Marston, Searle & Rivington, 1881.

Delacour, Jean. *The Living Air: The Memoirs of an Ornithologist.* London: Country Life, 1966.

Doherty, Peter. *Their Fate Is Our Fate: How Birds Foretell Threats to Our Health and Our World.* New York: The Experiment, 2013.

Elliott, Sara M. Quoted in Anne Raver, "When Birds Migrate, Central Park Is the Spot."

Elphick, Jonathan. *Birds: The Art of Ornithology*. London: Scriptum Editions, 2008.

Fisher, James, and Roger Tory Peterson. *The World of Birds*. London: Macdonald, 1964.

Franzen, Jonathan. "Emptying the Skies." *The New Yorker*, 07/26/2010.

——— *Freedom*. New York: Farrar, Straus, Giroux, 2010.

Freethy, Ron. *How Birds Work: A Guide to Bird Biology*. Poole: Blandford Press, 1982.

Gallagher, Tim. *The Grailbird: The Rediscovery of the Ivory-Billed Woodpecker*. Boston, New York: Houghton Mifflin, 2006.

——— *Imperial Dreams: Tracking the Imperial Woodpecker through the Wild Sierra Madre*. New York: Atria Books, 2013.

Garfield, Brian. *The Meinertzhagen Mystery: The Life and Legend of a Colossal Fraud*. Dulles: Potomac Books, 2007.

Gebhardt, Ludwig. *Die Ornithologen Mitteleuropas*. Wiebelsheim: Aula-Verlag, 2006.

Gentile, Olivia. *Life List: A Woman's Quest for the World's Most Amazing Birds*. New York: Bloomsbury, 2009.

Grant, Peter and Rosemary. Quoted in Jonathan Weiner, *The Beak of the Finch*.

Greenberg, Joel. *A Feathered River across the Sky: The Passenger Pigeon's Flight to Extinction*. New York: Bloomsbury, 2014.

Hahn, Paul. *Where Is That Vanished Bird? An Index to the Known Specimens of Extinct North American Species*. Toronto: Royal Ontario Museum, 1963.

Hanson, Thor. *Feathers: The Evolution of a Natural Miracle*. New York: Basic Books, 2013.

Harrison, Beatrice. Quoted in Jeremy Mynott, *Birdscapes*.

Head, Vernon R.L. *The Rarest Bird in the World: The Search for the Nechisar Nightjar*. New York: Pegasus Books, 2016.

Howard, Len. *Birds as Individuals*. London: Collins, 1953.

Hübner, Jacob. *Sammlung auserlesener Vögel und Schmetterlinge mit ihren Namen.* Augsburg: 1793. Description of Hübner from Ludwig Gebhardt, *Die Ornithologen Mitteleuropas.*

Juniper, Tony. *Spix's Macaw.* New York: Atria, 2003.

Kallio, Harri. *Der Dodo auf Mauritius. Die Wiedergeburt eines ausgestorbenen Vogels.* Berlin: Edition Braus im Wachter Verlag, 2004.

Karpinski, Jan. *Capital of Happiness.* London: Michael Joseph, 1984.

Kaufman, Kenn. *Kingbird Highway: The Biggest Year in the Life of an Extreme Birder.* New York: Houghton Mifflin, 1997. Quotes from the afterword to the 2006 edition.

Kinzelbach, Ragnar K., and Jochen Hölzinger. *Marcus zum Lamm (1544–1606): Die Vogelbücher aus dem Thesaurus Picturarum.* Stuttgart: Ulmer, 2000.

Kricher, John C. *Galápagos: A Natural History.* Princeton: Princeton University Press, 2006.

Lloyd, Clare. *The Travelling Naturalists.* London: Croom Helm, 1985.

Lorenz, Konrad. "Der Kumpan in der Umwelt des Vogels—Der Artgenosse als Auslöser sozialer Verhaltensweisen." *Journal für Ornithologie,* 2 (April 1935).

Macdonald, Helen. *H Is for Hawk.* London: Jonathan Cape, 2014.

Magenau, Jörg. *Brüder unterm Sternenzelt–Friedrich Georg und Ernst Jünger: Eine Biographie.* Stuttgart: Klett-Cotta, 2012.

Marzluff, John. *In the Company of Crows and Ravens.* New Haven: Yale University Press, 2005.

Mearns, Barbara, and Richard Mearns. *Biographies of Birdwatchers: The Lives of Those Commemorated in Western Palearctic Bird Names.* London: Academic Press, 1988.

——— *The Bird Collectors.* London: Academic Press, 1998.

Meyen, Franz Johann Friedrich. Quoted in Ludwig Gebhardt, *Die Ornithologen Mitteleuropas.*

Michelet, Jules. *The Bird.* London: T. Nelson and Sons, 1868.

Moss, Stephen. *A Bird in the Bush: A Social History of Birdwatching*. London: Aurum, 2005.

Mynott, Jeremy. *Birdscapes: Birds in Our Imagination and Experience*. Princeton: Princeton University Press, 2009.

Nice, Margaret Morse. *Research Is a Passion With Me: The Autobiography of a Bird Lover*. Toronto: Consolidated Amethyst Communications, 1979.

Oggins, Robin S. *The Kings and Their Hawks: Falconry in Medieval England*. New Haven: Yale University Press, 2004.

Oken, Lorenz. *Allgemeine Naturgeschichte für alle Stände. Siebenter Band erste Abtheilung, oder Thierreich vierter Band erste Abtheilung. Vögel*. Stuttgart: Hoffmann, 1837.

Pepperberg, Irene. *Alex and Me: How a Scientist and a Parrot Discovered a Hidden World of Animal Intelligence—and Formed a Deep Bond in the Process*. New York: HarperCollins, 2008.

Pigafetta, Antonio. *The First Voyage around the World, by Magellan*, translated by Lord Stanley of Alderley. London: Hakluyt Society, 1874.

Preuss, Niels Otto. "Hans Christian Cornelius Mortensen: Aspects of His Life and of the History of Bird Ringing." *Ardea*, *89*(1) (special edition 2001), pp. 1–6.

Raver, Anne. "When Birds Migrate, Central Park Is the Spot." *The New York Times*, 10/16/1994.

Reblin, Klaus. *Franziskus von Assisi: Der rebellische Bruder*. Göttingen: Vandenhoeck & Ruprecht, 2006.

Roberts, Sonia. *Bird Keeping and Birdcages*. Newton Abbot: David & Charles Publishers, 1972.

Rosen, Jonathan. *The Life of the Skies: Birding at the End of Nature*. New York: Picador, 2008.

Rothenberg, David. *Why Birds Sing: A Journey into the Mystery of Birdsong*. New York: Basic Books, 2005.

Rothschild, Lord Walter. *Extinct Birds: An Attempt to Unite in One Volume a Short Account of Those Birds Which Have Become Extinct in Historical Times*. London: Hutchinson & Co., 1907.

Rubinstein, Julian. "Operation Easter: The Hunt for Illegal Egg Collectors." *The New Yorker*, 07/22/2013.

Russ, Karl. *Die fremdländischen Stubenvögel*. Hannover: Carl Rümpler, 1879–88.

Salvadori, Giovanni. Quoted in Ludwig Gebhardt, *Die Ornithologen Mitteleuropas*.

Schmalkalden, Caspar. *Die wundersamen Reisen des Caspar Schmalkalden nach West- und Ostindien 1642–52*. Leipzig: F. A. Brockhaus Verlag, 1989.

Schneider, Bernhard. *Als die Wellensittiche nach Europa kamen: Auf den Spuren von Karl Ruß und Karl Neunzig—ein Streifzug durch 100 Jahre Geschichte der Vogelliebhaberei*. Berlin: self-published, 2005.

Seabrook, John. "Ruffled Feathers: Uncovering the Biggest Scandal in the Bird World." *The New Yorker*, 05/29/2006.

Secord, James A. "Nature's Fancy: Charles Darwin and the Breeding of Pigeons." *Isis*, 72(2) (June 1981), pp. 162–86.

Seebohm, Henry. *Siberia in Europe: A Visit to the Valley of the Petchora, in North-East Russia*. London: John Murray, 1880.

Selous, Edward. *Bird Watching*. London: Dent, 1901.

Sheldrake, Rupert, and Aimée Morgana. "Testing a Language: Using Parrot for Telepathy." *Journal of Scientific Exploration*, 17(4) (2003).

Snethlage, Heinrich. "Dr. Emilie Snethlage zum Gedächtnis." *Journal für Ornithologie*, 1930.

Stimmelmayr, Alex. "Über das kosmische Problem des Vogelzuges." *Mitteilungen über die Vogelwelt*. 33 (1934), pp. 49–57.

Stresemann, Erwin. *Ornithology: From Aristotle to the Present*. Cambridge: Harvard University Press, 1975.

Stroud, Patricia Tyson. *The Emperor of Nature: Charles-Lucien Bonaparte and His World*. Philadelphia: University of Pennsylvania Press, 2000.

Tate, Peter. *Birds, Men and Books: A Literary History of Ornithology*. London: Henry Sotheran, 1986.

Thoreau, Henry David. *Thoreau on Birds* (compiled by Helen Cruickshank). New York: McGraw-Hill, 1964.

Tudge, Colin. *The Secret Life of Birds: Who They Are and What They Do.* London: Penguin, 2009.

Verney, Peter. *Homo Tyrannicus: Vom gnadenlosen Kampf gegen Tiere.* Hannover: Landbuch-Verlag, 1981.

Videler, John J. *Avian Flight.* Oxford: Oxford University Press, 2005.

Walter, Adolf. "Meine Ohreule." *Monatsschrift des Deutschen Vereins zum Schutze der Vogelwelt, 12* (1887), pp. 162–75.

Walters, Michael. *A Concise History of Ornithology.* New Haven: Yale University Press, 2003.

Waterton, Charles. *Wanderings in South America, the North-West of the United States, and the Antilles.* London: Macmillan, 1885.

Weidensaul, Scott. *Living on the Wind: Across the Hemisphere with Migratory Birds.* New York: North Point Press, 1999.

Weigold, Hugo. "Ein Monat Ornithologie in den Wüsten und Kulturoasen Nordwestmesopotamiens und Innersyriens." *Journal für Ornithologie, 60* (July 1912), pp. 365–410.

Weiner, Jonathan. *The Beak of the Finch: A Story of Evolution in Our Time.* New York: Vintage Books, 1995.

Welker, Robert Henry. *Birds and Men: American Birds in Science, Art, Literature, and Conservation, 1800-1900.* Cambridge: Belknap Press, Harvard University, 1955.

Wendt, Herbert. *Auf Noahs Spuren: Die Entdeckung der Tiere.* Hamm: G. Grote'sche Verlagshandlung, 1956.

West, Meredith J., and Andrew P. King. "Mozart's Starling." *American Scientist, 78*(2) (March/April 1990), pp. 106–14.

White, T.H. *The Goshawk.* London: Jonathan Cape, 1951.

Wilson, Alexander. *American Ornithology, with notes by Jardine.* Boston: Otis, Broaders, and Company, 1840.

List of Illustrations

Unless otherwise mentioned, illustrations are in the public domain and reproduced from the holdings of the Museum für Naturkunde— Leibniz Institute for Evolution and Biodiversity Science, Berlin.

Jacket: *Sclater's Cassowary* by John Gerrard Keulemans. In Lionel Walter Rothschild, *Monograph of the Genus Casuarius*. London: Zoological Society of London, 1900.

Frontispiece*: Juan Fernández Firecrown.* In René Primevère Lesson, *Histoire naturelle des oiseaux-mouches.* Paris: Arthus Bertrand, 1829–30.

vi. Man with a bird. In Ernest Harold Baynes, *Wild Bird Guests and How to Entertain Them.* New York: E. P. Dutton & Company, 1915.

ix. *Aracari.* In François Levaillant, *Histoire naturelle des toucans et des barbus.* Paris: Denné & Perlot, 1801–06.

Facing 1. *Common Ground-Dove.* In Jean Théodore Descourtilz, *Oiseaux brillans du Brésil.* A. Zwemmer, 1834.

3. Woman at window with swifts. In Jules Michelet, *Die Welt der Vögel.* Berlin: Sacco, 1870.

5. Man listening to birds. Eighteenth-century woodcut. Archive of the author.

6. *Quetzals.* In John Gould, *A Monograph of the Trogonidae, or Family of Trogons.* London: published by the author, [1858]–1875.

8. Man with falcons. Single plate. Archive of the author.

9. Frederick II of Hohenstaufen with falcon. In *De arte venandi cum avibus.* From a manuscript in Biblioteca Vaticana, Pal. lat 1071, late thirteenth century. Wikimedia Commons.

11. Man with bird. In Carl Friedrich Flögel, *Geschichte der komischen Literatur.* Liegnitz, 1784–87.

12. Falconers in Abu Dhabi. With kind permission of Helen Macdonald.

14–15. *Crane.* In Conrad Gesner, *Vogel-Buch.* Frankfurt am Main: Wilhelm Serlin, 1669.

17. *Crane.* In Conrad Gesner, *Vogel-Buch.* Frankfurt am Main: Wilhelm Serlin, 1669.

18. *Mummified Birds of Paradise.* In John Jonston, *Histoire Naturelle et Raisonnée des differents oiseaux qui habitent le globe.* Paris: Chez L.C. Desnos, 1772–74. The book was originally published in 1772–74 with black-and-white engravings; these colored plates are from a later edition.

20. *Le Nebuleux Bird of Paradise.* In Robert Havell, *A Collection of the Birds of Paradise.* London: R. Havell, 1835.

22–23. Manucode. In Ullise Aldrovandi, *Ornithologiae.* Bologna: Francesco de Franceschi, 1599.

24. *Red-tailed Comet.* In René Primevère Lesson, *Histoire naturelle des oiseaux-mouches.* Paris: Arthus Bertrand, 1829–30.

27. *Helmetcrest Hummingbirds.* In Alfred E. Brehm, *Brehms Tierleben.* Leipzig und Wien: Bibliographisches Institut, 1891.

28. *Hummingbirds.* In Ernest Haeckel, *Kunstformen der Natur.* Leipzig und Wien: Verlag des Bibliographischen Instituts, 1899–1904.

30. *Cuban Amazon.* In François Levaillant, *Histoire Naturelle des Perroquets.* Paris: Levrault frères and Levrault, Schoell & Co., 1801–05.

34. Meinertzhagen with a kori bustard in Nairobi (1915). Wikimedia Commons.

37. *Forest Owlet*. In R.B. Sharpe, *The Scientific Results of the Yarkand Mission*. London: Eyre and Spottiswoode, 1891.

40. *Wilson's Bird of Paradise*. In John Gould, *The Birds of New Guinea and the Adjacent Papuan Islands, including many new species recently discovered in Australia*. London: H. Sotheran, 1875–88.

43. *Flamingo*. In Mark Catesby, *Natural History of Carolina, Florida and the Bahama Islands*. London: printed at the expense of the author, 1729–47.

44. Charles Lucien Bonaparte. Wikimedia Commons.

46. *Paradiesvögel* (Birds of paradise). *Brockhaus Konversations-Lexikon*. Leipzig, Berlin, Wien: F.A. Brockhaus, 1894. Archive of the author.

49. *John James Audubon* by John Syme, 1826. Wikimedia Commons.

50. *Great Horned Owl*. In John James Audubon, *Birds of America*. Edinburgh and London: published by the author, 1827–38.

53. *Red-tailed Comets*. In John Gould, *A Monograph of the Trochilidae, or Family of Humming-Birds*. London: published by the author, 1861.

56. *Il Barbaggiani* by Valentine Cameron Prinsep. Courtesy of the Art Renewal Center® www.artrenewal.org.

59. *Budgerigars*. In Alfred E. Brehm, *Brehms Tierleben*. Leipzig und Wien: Bibliographisches Institut, 1891.

60. Pet birds. In Karl Russ, *Die fremdländischen Stubenvögel*. Hannover: Carl Rümpler, 1879–88.

64–65. Karl Russ's "bird room." In Karl Russ, *Bilder aus der Vogelstube. Schilderungen aus dem Leben fremdländischer und einheimischer Stubenvögel*. Magdeburg: Creutz'sche Verlagsbuchhandlung, 1882.

66. *Redpolls (male and female)*. In Eleazar Albin, *Histoire Naturelle des Oiseaux*. The Hague: Pierre de Hondt, 1750.

68. *Cuban Amazon*. In Jacob Hübner, *Sammlung auserlesener Vögel und Schmetterlinge*. Augsburg, 1793. Courtesy of Universitätsbibliothek Heidelberg.

69. *Male Ruff*. In Marcus zum Lamm, *Thesaurus Pictuarum* (ca. 1600). Courtesy of Hessische Landes- und Hochschulbibliothek, Darmstadt.

70. *Landscape with Birds* by Roelandt Savery (1628). Wikimedia Commons.

72.Woman with bird on her hat. In Ernest Harold Baynes, *Wild Bird Guests: How to Entertain Them.* New York: E. P. Dutton & Company, 1915.

75. Wall painting in Assisi by Maestro di S. Francesco (ca. 1236). Archive of the author.

76. Henry David Thoreau. Wikimedia Commons.

79. *Louisiana Heron, Pied Oystercatcher, Whooping Crane, Long Billed Curlew.* In Alexander Wilson, *American ornithology, or, The natural history of the birds of the United States.* New York: Collins & Co., 1812.

82. Cerulean warbler. Rondeau Provincial Park, Ontario, Canada. Wikimedia Commons.

88. *African Grey Parrot.* In François Levaillant, *Histoire Naturelle des Oiseaux d'Afrique.* Paris: J.J. Fuchs, Delachaussée, 1805–08.

91. *Top:* Man with Reeve's pheasant. Vintage postcard. Archive of the author. *Bottom:* Scenes from a farm and garden with birds. In V.A. Jäger and G.A. Riecke, *Anleitung zum Unterricht taubstummer Kinder.* Stuttgart: Beck und Fränkel, 1831–36.

94. *Landhühner* (Country fowl). In Lorenz Oken, *Allgemeine Naturgeschichte für alle Stände.* Stuttgart: Hoffmann, 1843.

97. Magdalena Heinroth with owl. In Oskar and Magdalena Heinroth, *Die Vögel Mitteleuropas.* Berlin: Hugo Bermühler, 1924–34.

100. *Greylag Geese.* In Alfred E. Brehm, *Brehms Tierleben.* Leipzig und Wien: Bibliographisches Institut, 1892.

104. *Papageien* (Parrots). In Gotthilf Heinrich von Schubert, *Naturgeschichte der Vögel.* Esslingen: Schreiber, 1886.

105. *Specht* (Woodpeckers). In Gotthilf Heinrich von Schubert, *Naturgeschichte der Vögel.* Esslingen: Schreiber, 1886.

109. *Top: Cassowary. Bottom: Parrot* (called here "West-Indian Raven"). In Caspar Schmalkalden, *Die wundersamen Reisen des Caspar Schmalkalden nach West- und Ostindien 1642–52.* Leipzig: F.A. Brockhaus Verlag, 1989.

112. *Taubenartige Vögel* (Pigeonlike birds). In Gotthilf Heinrich von Schubert, *Naturgeschichte der Vögel.* Esslingen: Schreiber, 1886.

115. Pigeon photographed by Can Akgümüş. Eastern Turkey. Archive of the author.

116. Pigeon-keeping in Persia. Historical single plate. Archive of the author.

119. *Owl*. In Jacob Christian Schaeffer, *Elementa Ornithologica*. Regensburg, 1774.

122. *Spotted owl*. In Spencer F. Baird, *The Birds of North America*. Philadelphia: J.B. Lippincott & Co., 1860.

124–25. *Hawk*. In Alfred E. Brehm, *Brehms Tierleben*. Leipzig und Wien: Bibliographisches Institut, 1892.

126. *Humboldt Penguin*. In R.A. Philippi, *Anales del Museo Nacional de Chile. Primeira Seccion. Zoolojia*. Santiago de Chile: el Museo, 1902.

128–29. *Australian Little Penguins*. In John Gould, *The Birds of Australia*. London: published by the author, 1848.

130. *Rabenartige Vögel* (Ravenlike birds). In Gotthilf Heinrich von Schubert, *Naturgeschichte der Vögel*. Esslingen: Schreiber, 1886.

132–33. *Finches from the Galapagos*. In Charles Darwin, *Journal of Researches into the Natural History and Geology of the countries visited during the voyage of H.M.S. Beagle round the world*. London: John Murray, 1845.

134. *Alpine Swift*. In Alfred E. Brehm, *Brehms Tierleben*. Leipzig und Wien: Bibliographisches Institut, 1892.

139. *Red-naped Falcon*. In John Gould, *Birds of Asia*. London: published by the author, 1850.

140. *Die Töchter des Malers im türkischen Kostüm* (The Artist's Daughters in Turkish Costume) by Johann Heinrich Tischbein (detail). Courtesy of Freies Deutsches Hochstift/Frankfurter Goethe-Museum.

143. *Finches*. In Alfred E. Brehm, *Brehms Tierleben*. Leipzig und Wien: Bibliographisches Institut, 1892.

146. *Lyrebird*. In Alfred E. Brehm, *Brehms Tierleben*. Leipzig und Wien: Bibliographisches Institut, 1892.

149. *Straußenartige oder Laufvögel* (Ostrichlike birds or running birds). In Gotthilf Heinrich von Schubert, *Naturgeschichte der Vögel*. Esslingen: Schreiber, 1886.

198. *Major Mitchell's Cockatoo.* In John Gould, *A Synopsis of the Birds of Australia, and the Adjacent Islands.* London: published by the author, 1837–38.

201. Roxie Laybourne photographed by Chip Clark. Reproduced with kind permission of Smithsonian Institution.

202. Wing and tail feathers. In Jacob Christian Schaeffer, *Elementa Ornithologica.* Regensburg, 1774.

204. *Arctic Tern.* Single plate, twentieth century. Archive of the author.

207. *Common Cuckoos.* In Johann Andreas and Johann Friedrich Naumann, *Die Naturgeschichte der Vögel Mitteleuropas.* Gera: Köhler, 1897.

208. Margaret Morse Nice. Wikipedia Commons.

213. *Kiwis.* In Alfred E. Brehm, *Brehms Tierleben.* Leipzig und Wien: Bibliographisches Institut, 1892.

214–15. Bird heads and feet. In Jacob Christian Schaeffer, *Elementa Ornithologica.* Regensburg, 1774.

218–19. *Little Owl.* In Alfred E. Brehm, *Brehms Tierleben.* Leipzig und Wien: Bibliographisches Institut, 1892.

222: *Sclater's Cassowary* by John Gerrard Keulemans. In Lionel Walter Rothschild, *Monograph of the Genus Casuarius.* London: Zoological Society of London, 1900.

225. *Dodo.* In Mariotti Giovanni, *Das Bestiarium des Aloys Zötl.* Genf: Weber, 1980.

227. *Apterornis coerulescens.* In Lionel Walter Rothschild, *Extinct Birds.* London: Hutchinson, 1907.

230. *Passenger pigeons.* In Heinrich Gottlieb Ludwig Reichenbach, *Handbuch der speciellen Ornithologie.* Dresden und Leipzig, 1850.

233. *Ivory-billed Woodpecker.* In Alexander Wilson, *American ornithology, or, The natural history of the birds of the United States.* New York: Collins & Co., 1818–29.

236. *Red-crested Cardinal.* In Jean Théodore Descourtilz, *Oiseaux brillans du Brésil.* Paris, 1834.

239. Ludwig Koch. Archive of the author.

Index of Birds

Numbers in italics indicate illustrations

Index of People

Numbers in italics indicate illustrations